The Daily Telegraph Book of Breads, Cakes & Puddings

D1350677

BY THE SAME AUTHOR

QUICK COOK

THANE PRINCE

The Daily Telegraph
BREADS, CAKES & PUDDINGS

Chatto & Windus
LONDON

Published in 1992 by
Chatto & Windus Ltd
20 Vauxhall Bridge Road
London SW1V 2SA

A CIP Catalogue record for this book is
available from the British Library.

ISBN 0 7011 3844 0

Design by Margaret Sadler
Illustrations by Diana Leadbetter
Photoset by Rowland Phototypesetting Ltd,
Bury St Edmunds, Suffolk
Printed in Great Britain by
Butler and Tanner Ltd,
Frome and London

Contents

*For my father, Tom Hurry, who has enjoyed
a lifelong dedication to cakes and puddings.*

Acknowledgements

Firstly I must thank Margaret Kenwood at
The Daily Telegraph for the endless help
she has given me with all these recipes.
Thanks also to the rest of the *Telegraph*'s
Weekend team, who continue to support me
with encouragement and friendship. To
Linda Sonntag, whom I was lucky enough
to have edit this book as well as my first,
Quick Cook. To my family and all the
neighbours who have valiantly eaten their
way through mountains of cakes and buns.
And finally to everyone at Chatto &
Windus, especially Katie White and Rowena
Skelton-Wallace, who have been unfailingly
helpful and optimistic.

Introduction

I HAVE TO admit that my motives for wanting to write a book about breads, cakes and puddings are purely self-indulgent. I love sticky cakes, homemade bread and luscious puddings, and to have to cook them and eat them for my work is my idea of bliss. It has also made me lots of friends. Almost overnight I became very popular with the neighbouring boys, and as the cakes and puddings stacked up I was thrilled with Alfie and Bill's dedicated and enthusiastic help in eating them once my family could eat no more.

When I began to write cake and pudding recipes for the *Telegraph*, I had no idea how popular they would become. Everyone enjoys the comfort of a hot pudding, and the luxury of a dessert oozing chocolate and cream, and few can resist a slice of freshly baked homemade cake with a cup of tea, but in this age of rush and bustle, were people still prepared to bake at home?

My doubts were quickly dispelled. The huge response in my postbag showed that not only is cake and pudding making as popular as ever, but that many of my readers are also rediscovering the delights of baking their own bread.

The recipes in this book will, I hope, give further encouragement, as they are all simple, as well as utterly delicious. All you have to do is follow them exactly, paying particular attention to the weighing of ingredients, which is crucial in any form of baking. Stick to either the imperial or the metric measurements. Weights and measures have been rounded off to a standard conversion table, except where doing so would favour the mathematician at the expense of the cook.

The proof, as they say, will be in the eating. You don't need to eat these heavenly foods every day, but when they come fresh from your own oven, I can promise you that the taste will be unbeatable.

CHAPTER
1
Cakes

I WONDER WHEN the very first cake was baked and what it looked and tasted like? I suppose it must have been a flat patty of roughly ground flour and water cooked on a bake stone, and I don't doubt that with the first bite of this hot cake the caveman realized that here was a discovery at least as important as the wheel.

The Romans loved wheat cakes made with honey, the Chinese favoured rice flour. King Alfred burnt the cakes and Marie Antoinette, rather foolishly as it turned out, suggested that the French peasants should eat cake instead of bread!

Cakes today are found at celebrations as well as on the family tea table, for cakes are special. Can you imagine a wedding without an intricately decorated many-tiered cake? Cakes take time to make, and they are made from good things not actually necessary in the daily diet. Speak to anyone who has lived through food rationing with its limited allowance of eggs and sugar and you will soon discover how much of a treat cakes really are.

Cake has inspired poets and writers alike. The evocative taste of madeleines, little light sponges baked in a traditional shell mould, inspired Proust to write his epic novel *Remembrance of Things Past*. Byron loved the richly spiced gingerbread traditionally sold at hiring fairs along with brandy snaps, and still to be found on the sweet stalls of amusement fairs that mark the seasons of British life.

Few things look more tempting than big cakes sitting proudly on cake stands waiting to be cut. Chocolate cakes with glossy icing, lemon sponges filled with tangy lemon curd, coconut cakes, carrot cakes, old-fashioned seed cakes and newly popular courgette cakes: this chapter has cakes to suit all comers.

Small cakes are particular favourites with children at teatime, ideal with a cup of coffee mid-morning or afternoon, and pack conveniently into lunch and picnic boxes. Some are made in large tins and cut into bars or slices, others are made in tart or bun tins or paper cake cases. Small cakes begin on page 26.

All these cakes are simple to make and they all keep well in an airtight tin . . . if they're allowed to.

There are almost as many different types of cake as there are cooks, but some basic principles apply to all baking. With cake making more than any other form of cooking it is vitally important to measure the ingredients accurately. The ratio of fat, sugar and flour to liquid is critical to the finished result, and while an extra spoonful of syrup in a pie filling won't harm the pie, the same generous quantity in a cake will give a forlorn and flat result that leaves everyone disappointed.

☐ Weigh all ingredients carefully.

☐ All ingredients should be at room temperature.

☐ Use level spoon measures unless otherwise specified.

☐ Warm syrup or honey before measuring to get exact results.

☐ Use size 2 eggs unless otherwise stated.

☐ Even the smallest speck of yolk will stop egg white from forming a stiff foam when whipped, as will any trace of grease in the mixing bowl or on the whisk, so when making meringues, do wash all implements carefully before use.

☐ Preheat the oven according to the manufacturer's instructions. I have found that even when using a fan-assisted oven it is best to preheat when baking cakes or bread.

☐ Choose the correct size and type of tin for the recipe. I know that recipes always seem to call for a tin a centimetre or an inch larger or smaller than the one you have, and it is perfectly alright to use this as long as you remember that if your tin is larger than the size asked for, the mixture will spread to form a thinner cake which will take less time to cook. With a smaller than suggested tin the cake mixture will of course be deeper, and so will require a slightly longer cooking time.

☐ To convert a recipe for a round tin to one of a different shape, fill a tin of the recommended size with water and pour this into the tin you wish to use to check the volume.

☐ Don't remove the cake from the oven until it is fully cooked! When a cake is cooked it should be evenly brown, well risen and have started to pull away from the sides of the tin.

A tester (a fine skewer or toothpick) inserted into the centre of the cake should come out clean, i.e. with no raw cake mixture sticking to it.

When a cooked cake is lightly pressed with your fingertip, it springs back. If your fingertip makes an indentation, cook for a few minutes longer.

☐ Always allow the cake to sit in the tin to cool for about 10 minutes, unless otherwise stated, before carefully turning out on to a rack to cool completely.

☐ Ice cakes when they are cold unless told otherwise.

☐ Store cakes in an airtight tin.

CHOCOLATE ALMOND CAKE
with soured cream ganache icing

225 g/8 oz soft butter
115 g/4 oz soft brown sugar
115 g/4 oz caster sugar
3 size 2 eggs, beaten
115 g/4 oz plain chocolate
170 g/6 oz plain flour
2 teaspoons baking powder
60 g/2 oz ground almonds

to ice
115 g/4 oz plain chocolate pieces
140 ml/¼ pint soured cream
icing sugar for sprinkling

Beat the butter with the two sugars until light and fluffy. Add the egg a little at a time, beating well. Melt the chocolate in a bowl over a pan of simmering water and stir in. Sift in the flour with the baking powder and ground almonds and fold in.

Divide the batter between two 23 cm/9 inch greased and floured sandwich tins. Bake in a preheated oven at 180°C/360°F/Gas 4 for 30–35 minutes, until cooked.

Allow to cool for 5 minutes, remove from the tins, and allow to cool completely.

To make the ganache icing, melt the chocolate pieces and stir in the soured cream, mixing until glossy. You may need to keep the bowl over simmering water.

Sandwich the cooled layers together with the icing and sprinkle the top with icing sugar.

CHOCOLATE HAZELNUT RING
with coffee buttercream

125 g/4½ oz caster sugar
125 g/4½ oz soft margarine
2 size 2 eggs, beaten
115 g/4 oz self-raising flour
85 g/3 oz ground hazelnuts
60 g/2 oz chocolate, grated

to ice
60 g/2 oz soft butter
140 g/5 oz icing sugar, sifted
1 teaspoon instant coffee,
    dissolved in 1 teaspoon hot
    water

Cream the sugar and margarine until light and fluffy. Add the egg a little at a time, beating well after each addition. Mix together the flour, hazelnuts and chocolate, and fold in.

Spoon the batter into a greased, floured 23 cm/9 inch ring mould and bake in the centre of a preheated oven at 180°C/360°F/Gas 4 for 40–50 minutes, until the cake is well risen and a tester inserted in the centre comes out clean. Cool for 5 minutes before turning on to a rack.

When the cake is cold, slice carefully in half through the centre. Beat together the icing ingredients and use to sandwich the cake.

CHOCOLATE CAKE
with chocolate nut frosting

225 g/8 oz butter
4 tablespoons cocoa powder
220 ml/8 fl oz water
285 g/10 oz plain flour
340 g/12 oz caster sugar
140 ml/¼ pint soured cream
2 teaspoons baking powder
½ teaspoon vanilla essence
2 size 2 eggs, beaten

for the frosting
125 g/4½ oz butter
3 tablespoons milk
2 tablespoons cocoa powder
½ teaspoon vanilla essence
225 g/8 oz icing sugar, sifted
85 g/3 oz chopped nuts

This chocolate slab cake makes an excellent cake stall or cricket tea cake. It is easy to make, stays moist and freezes well.

Bring the butter, cocoa powder and water to the boil, mixing thoroughly. Pour this over the flour and sugar and beat well. Add the soured cream, baking powder and vanilla, then beat in the eggs. Pour the mixture into a shallow 33 × 20 cm/13 × 8 inch cake tin and bake in a preheated oven at 190°C/375°F/Gas 5 for 25–30 minutes, or until a tester inserted into the centre comes out clean.

While the cake cooks make the frosting. Melt the butter in the milk and beat in the cocoa powder. Bring up to the boil and beat in the remaining ingredients. Continue to beat for 2–3 minutes, and spread over the hot cake. Allow to cool before slicing.

CHOCOLATE FUDGE CAKE
with whipped cream

85 g/3 oz caster sugar
3 size 2 eggs
140 g/5 oz plain chocolate
140 ml/¼ pint soured cream
85 g/3 oz self-raising flour

to finish
2–3 tablespoons brandy or orange liqueur
180 ml/⅓ pint cream, whipped

With an electric mixer whisk the sugar and eggs to a thick white foam. Meanwhile, melt the chocolate in a bowl over simmering water and stir in the soured cream, mixing well. Sift the flour.

Have ready a greased, floured 20 cm/8 inch cake tin, and preheat the oven to 200°C/400°F/Gas 6.

Sift the flour again, over the foam, and pour on the chocolate mixture. Very carefully cut and fold the mixture until everything is combined. Pour into the prepared tin and bake in the oven for 25 minutes.

Remove and allow to cool. The cake will sink slightly and the surface may crack a little.

Once the cake has cooled, turn it on to a serving dish. Make a few holes in it with a cocktail stick, then sprinkle on the brandy. Pile whipped cream on the cake and serve.

CHOCOLATE BISCUIT CAKE

400 g/14 oz broken biscuits
85 g/3 oz slivered blanched
** almonds**
85 g/3 oz glacé cherries, halved
2 eggs
2 tablespoons caster sugar
170 g/6 oz butter
115 g/4 oz plain chocolate

About two or three times a year I notice that my biscuit barrel has rather more bits in it than whole biscuits. So, ever thrifty, I make this chocolate cake with the pieces. I use raw egg as this gives a wonderfully rich cake, but if you prefer, you could substitute 4–5 tablespoons fresh orange juice.

Put the biscuits into a large bowl, and break into 1 cm/½ inch pieces. Add the cherries and the nuts.

Beat the eggs with the caster sugar and strain over the biscuits, then toss everything together. If using orange juice, add it with the sugar. Melt the butter and chocolate over a low heat, stirring well. Pour the hot liquid over the biscuit mixture, and mix thoroughly.

Spoon the cake into a loaf tin, level the top and place in the fridge for 2–3 hours to set.

To unmould, dip the tin into hot water for 15 seconds, then turn on to a plate. Cut into thin slices to serve.

CHOCOLATE CHIP POUND CAKE

115 g/4 oz soft margarine or butter
170 g/6 oz caster sugar
½ teaspoon vanilla essence
2 size 2 eggs, beaten
170 g/6 oz self-raising flour
140 ml/¼ pint single cream
115 g/4 oz plain chocolate chips

Cream the butter, sugar and vanilla, mixing until pale and light. Beat in the egg a little at a time. Once all the egg has been added, fold in the flour and cream. Fold in the chocolate chips and spoon the batter into a large greased loaf tin. Bake the cake in a preheated oven at 180°C/360°F/Gas 4 for 45–55 minutes, or until well risen, golden brown and pulling slightly from the sides of the tin.

Allow to cool for 15 minutes before removing from the tin to a wire rack.

CHERRY, CHOCOLATE AND LEMON PATCHWORK CAKE

170 g/6 oz butter
170 g/6 oz caster sugar
3 size 3 eggs, beaten
170 g/6 oz self-raising flour
1 tablespoon cocoa powder
60 g/2 oz chocolate chips
45 g/1½ oz chopped glacé cherries
a few drops of pink food colouring
1 teaspoon grated lemon rind
1 tablespoon lemon juice

Perfect for a picnic tea, this loaf cake cuts into colourful slices, each mouthful having a different flavour.

Cream the butter and sugar until light and fluffy, then add the beaten egg a little at a time. Should the mixture curdle, stir in a tablespoon of flour. Fold in the flour, then divide the batter into three equal portions in individual bowls.

Into one bowl mix the cocoa powder and chocolate chips, into the next the cherries and pink colouring, and into the last the lemon rind and juice.

Have ready a greased and floured 725 g/1½ lb loaf tin. Spoon the mixtures into the tin, putting in random spoonfuls of each colour until you have used all the mix. Bake the cake in a preheated oven at 180°C/360°F/ Gas 4 for 50–60 minutes, or until well risen and beginning to pull slightly from the sides of the tin. Allow to cool on a rack.

ONE-BOWL CHOCOLATE FLAKE CAKE

with honey icing

115 g/4 oz soft margarine
115 g/4 oz self-raising flour
2 size 3 eggs
115 g/4 oz selfraising flour
1 level teaspoon baking powder
45 g/1½ oz chocolate flakes or grated chocolate

for the honey frosting
2 tablespoons margarine
1 tablespoon thick honey
4 tablespoons icing sugar

My daughter Amber invented this cake one damp Sunday afternoon.

Preheat the oven to 180°C/360°F/ Gas 4. Have a 450 g/1 lb loaf tin ready greased and floured.

Place all the ingredients in a bowl and beat well. Put the mixture into the tin and bake for 30–40 minutes, until well risen and golden brown.

Remove from the oven, cool for 5 minutes, then remove from the tin and cool on a rack.

Beat together the frosting ingredients and spread on the cold cake.

GÂTEAU AUX NOIX

170 g/6 oz butter, softened
170 g/6 oz caster sugar
225 g/8 oz finely chopped walnuts
2 eggs, separated
85 g/3 oz plain flour
2 tablespoons rum

for the chocolate ganache icing
125 g/4½ oz plain chocolate
2 tablespoons double cream

In a large bowl, mix together the butter, sugar, nuts, egg yolks, flour and rum, and blend well. In a separate bowl, beat the egg whites until stiff but not dry. Carefully fold the whites into the nut mixture and pour the batter into a greased, floured 23 cm/9 inch cake tin.

Bake in a preheated oven at 180°C/360°F/Gas 4 for 20–25 minutes, until the cake is browned and beginning to pull away from the sides of the tin. Turn on to a rack to cool.

To make the icing, melt the chocolate carefully and stir in the cream. Ice the cake at once.

SEED CAKE

170 g/6 oz butter
170 g/6 oz caster sugar
3 eggs, beaten
170 g/6 oz self-raising flour
a squeeze of lemon juice
1–2 tablespoons caraway seeds

Cream the butter with the sugar, and beat until pale and fluffy. Add the egg a little at a time, beating well, then fold in the flour, lemon juice and caraway seeds, mixing carefully until everything is well combined.

Pour into a greased loaf tin and bake in a preheated oven at 180°C/360°F/Gas 4 for 45–55 minutes, or until well risen and golden brown, and a tester inserted in the centre of the cake comes out clean. Cool on a rack.

Hazelnut and apricot roulade

3 size 2 eggs
115 g/4 oz caster sugar
½ teaspoon vanilla essence
30 g/1 oz self-raising flour
100 g/3½ oz ground hazelnuts

to fill
4–5 tablespoons apricot jam
275 ml/½ pint whipped cream

This can be made and filled the night before it is needed.

Line a Swiss roll pan with buttered, floured greaseproof paper. Preheat the oven to 200°C/400°F/Gas 6.

Whisk the eggs with the sugar and vanilla essence to a thick, pale foam. Mix together the flour and ground nuts, and fold carefully into the egg mixture.

Pour the mousse into the prepared tin, level the surface, and bake for 12–15 minutes. The cake should be well risen, light brown and just pulling away from the sides of the tin.

Have a large piece of greaseproof paper spread on the side and dust liberally with caster sugar. As soon as you remove the cake from the oven invert it on to the sugared paper. Allow it to cool for 2–3 minutes, then peel off the greaseproof. Cover the cake with a clean tea towel until cold.

To fill, spread the cake with jam and then cream. Using the paper to help, roll up the cake, starting from the long side closest to you. Press the cake gently into shape and trim the crispy ends. Don't worry if the cake cracks slightly, as this will show off the attractive filling. Place on a serving dish and refrigerate until needed.

STICKY GINGER CAKE

170 g/6 oz soft margarine
170 g/6 oz golden syrup
2 size 2 eggs, beaten
140 ml/5 fl oz/¼ pint milk
285 g/10 oz plain flour
1 teaspoon bicarbonate of soda
3 teaspoons ground ginger
½ teaspoon freshly grated nutmeg
1 teaspoon ground cinnamon
60 g/2 oz soft brown sugar
3 large pieces stem ginger, sliced
  into matchsticks
115 g/4 oz sultanas or chopped
  dates

Melt the margarine with the syrup, and allow to cool for 2–3 minutes. Beat the eggs into the milk. Sift together the flour, bicarbonate of soda and spices. Combine all the ingredients and pour the batter into a greased 20 cm/8 inch cake tin lined with greaseproof paper.

   Bake in a preheated oven at 180°C/360°F/Gas 4 for 50 minutes, or until a tester inserted in the centre comes out clean. Allow to cool.

STRAWBERRY HAZELNUT CREAM CAKE

3 size 3 eggs
85 g/3 oz caster sugar
½ teaspoon vanilla essence
1 teaspoon baking powder
30 g/1 oz plain flour
85 g/3 oz ground hazelnuts

for the topping
275 ml/½ pint whipping cream
2 tablespoons caster sugar
½ teaspoon vanilla essence
450 g/1 lb strawberries or other
  prepared fruit

This deliciously light sponge cake is topped with whipped cream and covered with fresh fruit. I use strawberries, but any summer fruit would be good.

Using an electric beater, beat the eggs, sugar and vanilla to a thick, firm foam. Sift the baking powder with the flour and mix with the nuts. Fold this carefully into the egg mixture with a metal spoon. Pour the mixture into a greased 23 cm/9 inch sponge tin lined with a piece of greaseproof paper in the base.

   Bake the cake in a preheated oven at 180°C/360°F/Gas 4 for 20–25 minutes, or until it pulls slightly from the sides of the tin. Allow to cool, then top with whipped sweetened cream flavoured with vanilla, and fruit.

TROPICAL FRUIT CAKE

425 g/15 oz self-raising flour
285 g/10 oz caster sugar
½ teaspoon salt
1 teaspoon cinnamon
3 size 2 eggs
330 ml/12 fl oz vegetable oil
½ teaspoon vanilla essence
255 g/9 oz chopped bananas
   (peeled weight)
115 g/4 oz chopped walnuts
400 g/14 oz tin crushed pineapple,
   drained

This moist cake can be iced with cream cheese frosting for high days and holidays.

In a large bowl, mix the flour, sugar, salt and spices together. Beat the eggs with the oil and vanilla essence. Combine all the ingredients and stir well. Pour the mixture into a greased 33 × 18 × 5 cm/13 × 9 × 2 inch tin and bake in a preheated oven at 180°C/360°F/Gas 4 for 50–55 minutes, or until light golden brown and pulling away from the sides of the tin.

   Allow to cool, then cut into bars and store in an airtight tin.

CRUNCHY LEMON CAKE

3 size 2 eggs
weight of the eggs in butter, caster
   sugar and self-raising flour
finely grated rind of 1 large, well
   scrubbed lemon

to finish
85 g/3 oz caster sugar
juice of the lemon

Here is a family favourite. Made using the basic sponge formula of the weight of the eggs in butter, sugar and flour, this cake is 'iced' with a lemon juice and sugar glaze poured over while it is still hot.

Cream the butter and sugar until light and fluffy. Beat the eggs and add a little at a time, beating well between each addition. Fold in the flour and lemon rind and spoon the batter into a greased, floured 725 g/1½ lb loaf tin.

   Bake the cake in a preheated oven at 180°C/360°F/Gas 4 for 50–60 minutes, until golden brown and well risen. The cake is done when it starts to pull away from the sides of the tin.

   Meanwhile, mix the remaining sugar into the lemon juice. You should have a thick pouring consistency. Give it a final stir, then pour over the hot cake. Ease the cake gently from the sides of the tin with a palette knife to allow the glaze to run down into the tin. Allow to cool, and remove from the tin when cold.

CLEMENTINE POUND CAKE

rind from 2 clementines
170 g/6 oz caster sugar
115 g/4 oz soft margarine
2 size 2 eggs, beaten
170 g/6 oz self-raising flour
3 tablespoons soured cream

to finish
140 ml/¼ pint water
2 tablespoons sugar
clementine segments
a squeeze of lemon juice

Pound cakes are usually rich in fat, and one recipe I have uses 12 egg yolks. This version is rather more restrained, and the cake is flavoured with the rind of the fruit and decorated with the segments.

In a food processor or blender finely grind the rind with the sugar. Tip into a large bowl, mix in the margarine, and beat until light and fluffy. Add the egg a little at a time, beating well after each addition. Fold in the flour and soured cream.

Pour the batter into a greased 725 g/1½ lb loaf tin and bake in a preheated oven at 180°C/360°F/ Gas 4 for 40–50 minutes, or until the cake pulls from the side of the tin and a tester, inserted in the centre, comes out clean.

Remove from the oven and allow to cool for 5 minutes, then remove from the tin.

Meanwhile, place the water and sugar in a small saucepan and bring to the boil, stirring to dissolve the sugar. Simmer the syrup over a low heat for 5 minutes. Strip any pith from the clementine segments, and add them. Simmer the fruit in the syrup over a medium heat until only about 2 tablespoons syrup remain. Stir in the lemon juice. Arrange the segments in a line along the top of the cake, and paint on the glaze with a pastry brush.

CRANBERRY AND PECAN COFFEE CAKE

170 g/6 oz plain flour
115 g/4 oz caster sugar
¼ teaspoon salt
1 teaspoon baking powder
1 size 3 egg, beaten
6 tablespoons milk
30 g/1 oz melted butter
115 g/4 oz fresh cranberries
115 g/4 oz chopped pecan nuts

for the topping
15 g/½ oz butter
30 g/1 oz plain flour
30 g/1 oz caster sugar
1 teaspoon cinnamon

In America, coffee cake is cake to be eaten with coffee, not flavoured with coffee. Cranberries give a wonderfully tart bite to this cake.

Mix together the flour, sugar, salt and baking powder. Beat the egg with the milk and add the butter. Add the milk mixture to the flour and mix to combine, then stir in the cranberries and nuts. Stir only until the ingredients are mixed, and do not beat.

Pour into a deep 18 cm/7 inch cake tin. Rub together the ingredients for the topping, and sprinkle over the top.

Bake the cake in a preheated oven at 180°C/360°F/Gas 4 for 25–30 minutes, or until a tester inserted in the centre comes out clean. Serve warm.

BLUEBERRY COFFEE CAKE

170 g/6 oz plain flour
85 g/3 oz caster sugar
1 teaspoon baking powder
½ teaspoon salt
1 egg
5 tablespoons milk
30 g/1 oz butter, melted
170–225 g/6–8 oz fresh blueberries

for the topping
30 g/1 oz plain flour
30 g/1 oz caster sugar
15 g/½ oz butter
1 teaspoon ground cinnamon

Fresh blueberries have made a relatively recent appearance in our shops. This coffee cake (i.e. cake to be eaten with coffee) makes the most of this delicious fruit.

Grease a 15 cm/6 inch loose bottomed deep cake tin.

Beat together all the cake ingredients except the berries until smooth. Carefully fold in the fruit, and spoon the mixture into the prepared tin.

Rub together the topping ingredients to make a crumble, and sprinkle over the cake batter.

Bake in a preheated oven at 190°C/375°F/Gas 5 for 50–55 minutes, until well risen and a tester inserted into the centre comes out clean. Allow to cool on a wire rack and store in an airtight tin.

BLACKBERRY AND APPLE UPSIDE-DOWN CAKE

30 g/1 oz butter
1 tablespoon golden syrup
2 small golden delicious apples,
**   peeled and diced**
170 g/6 oz fresh blackberries
125 g/4½ oz butter
125 g/4½ oz caster sugar
2 eggs, beaten
125 g/4½ oz self-raising flour
2 teaspoons ground cinnamon
1 tablespoon milk

This is a variation on the traditional pineapple cake. I prefer sharper tasting fresh blackberries to tinned pineapple.

Preheat the oven to 180°C/360°F/Gas 4.

Mix 30 g/1 oz butter with the syrup and spread over the base of a 20 cm/8 inch cake tin at least 5 cm/2 inches deep. Arrange the apples with the blackberries over the syrup mixture. Cream the remaining butter with the sugar, beat in the eggs, a little at a time, and fold in the flour and cinnamon. Add a little milk if the mixture is stiff.

Carefully spread the cake batter over the fruit and bake for 30–35 minutes, until well risen and golden brown. Remove from the oven and allow to sit for 5 minutes, then invert on to a plate. Let the tin sit on top of the cake for 2–3 minutes so all the juices run into the cake, then remove the tin and allow to cool. This cake is delicious served with clotted cream.

MARMALADE CRUMBLE CAKE

170 g/6 oz butter
340 g/12 oz self-raising flour, sifted
1 teaspoon baking powder
115 g/4 oz caster sugar
2 heaped tablespoons marmalade
2 medium eggs, beaten
milk to mix

for the topping
60 g/2 oz light muscovado sugar
1 teaspoon ground cinnamon

Delicious eaten warm from the oven with cream or vanilla ice, this cake has a crumbly cinnamon and brown sugar topping.

Rub the butter into the flour, baking powder and sugar. When the mixture resembles fine crumbs, reserve a quarter of it for the topping.

Mix the marmalade and eggs with the remaining mixture, adding milk if needed to give a soft dropping consistency. Pour the cake mixture into a prepared deep 20 cm/8 inch cake tin.

For the topping, mix the muscovado sugar and the cinnamon with the reserved crumbs, and sprinkle over. Bake the cake in a preheated oven at 180°C/360°F/Gas 4 for 50–60 minutes, until well risen and beginning to pull from the sides of the tin. Allow to cool slightly, then transfer to a rack.

Walnut cake

170 g/6 oz soft butter
170 g/6 oz caster sugar
3 size 3 eggs, beaten
170 g/6 oz self-raising flour
60 g/2 oz chopped walnuts

for the icing
5 tablespoons water
225 g/8 oz caster sugar
2 egg whites
5–6 walnut halves

It is said to be a sure sign of advanced age if you can remember Fuller's walnut cakes for tea. I remember them very well, and even recall being taken to tea at Fuller's Tea Rooms in London as a holiday treat. Now I think back with nostalgia to the shiny white box with its crest while I nibble on slices of my homemade version.

Cream the butter with the sugar and fold in the egg, a little at a time. Add the flour and then the walnuts, and pour the batter into three 15 cm/6 inch or two 20 cm/8 inch prepared sandwich tins. Bake in a preheated oven at 180°C/360°F/Gas 4, for 25–35 minutes, until risen and golden brown. Allow to cool on a rack.

To make the icing, put the water and sugar into a heavy saucepan and heat until the sugar has dissolved. Bring the syrup to the boil and boil rapidly for 3–5 minutes, until it leaves a fine thread when dropped from the spoon.

Beat the egg whites with an electric mixer until stiff. Add the hot syrup, still beating, and continue to beat the frosting until very stiff.

Use the frosting to sandwich the layers together, then cover the cake with the remainder. Decorate with walnut halves. The icing will set hard if left overnight.

OAT AND BROWN SUGAR CAKE
with nut frosting

85 g/3 oz porridge oats
275 ml/½ pint boiling water
115 g/4 oz butter
170 g/6 oz soft brown sugar
115 g/4 oz white sugar
2 eggs, beaten
1 teaspoon vanilla essence
200 g/7 oz wholemeal flour
1½ teaspoons baking powder
½ teaspoon salt
1½ teaspoons cinnamon
½ teaspoon nutmeg

for the frosting
30 g/1 oz butter, melted
85 g/3 oz soft brown sugar
3 tablespoons single cream
45 g/1½ oz chopped nuts
60 g/2 oz desiccated coconut

In the days before the invention of the eye-level grill, American settlers used a red hot 'peel' or shovel to cook the frosting on their special occasion cakes.

Mix the oats into the boiling water and allow it to soak while you prepare the other ingredients.

Cream the butter with the sugars until light and fluffy. Mix in the beaten egg a little at a time, and then add the vanilla. Now beat the oatmeal in well, making sure to break up any lumps. Sift in the flour with the baking powder, salt and spices, and fold quickly but thoroughly into the mixture. Pour the batter into a greased, floured 23 cm/9 inch springform tin and bake in a preheated oven at 180°C/360°F/Gas 4 for 45–50 minutes, until the cake is springy to the touch and has begun to pull slightly away from the sides of the tin.

Have the grill heated. Mix together the ingredients for the frosting. Spread the frosting over the hot cake and place under the well heated grill. Cook, turning if necessary, until the frosting bubbles and browns. Allow to cool, then remove from the tin.

FRIENDSHIP CAKE

When living in North America I was offered a pot of frothy cream and told it was a 'starter' for Friendship cake. Along with the jar came a list of seemingly complex instructions and a recipe.

The sourdough starter is grown in the fridge for 10 days and fed with flour, milk and sugar, then divided into four equal parts. With one part you make the cake, using any of a variety of flavourings; with the second you begin the process again; and the remaining two parts are given to friends, hence the name.

The finished cake is light and crumbly with a slight but distinctive sourdough flavour. When apples are in season it can be made with Bramleys, but it is just as good made with dried fruit during the winter, and my children love it with chocolate chips or banana and coconut. The cake is very simple to make and a great talking point. Portions of the base, with instructions, make an unusual addition to summer cake stalls.

You need to make the yeast-based mixture only once, then start again with the reserved portion of cake base. Should you not want to do this immediately, you can freeze the starter for up to three months.

for the sourdough starter
1½ teaspoons dried yeast
140 g/5 oz plain flour
220 ml/8 fl oz warm water

Mix the ingredients together. Cover the mixture and leave in a warm place, stirring daily, for 3 days, by which time it should be frothy and have a distinctive slightly sour fermented smell.

for the cake base
Take the starter as above, or the quarter portion of the cake base, and proceed as follows.
Day 1 Add 140 g/5 oz plain flour, 220 ml/8 fl oz milk and 85 g/3 oz sugar. Mix well, cover and refrigerate.
Days 2, 3, 4 Stir and return to the fridge.
Day 5 Repeat day 1, transferring the mixture to a larger bowl.
Days 6, 7, 8, 9 Stir and return to the fridge.
Day 10 Divide into 4 equal parts.

for the cake
1 part of the base
225 g/8 oz plain flour
225 g/8 oz sugar (or less)
220 ml/8 fl oz vegetable oil
2 teaspoons/baking powder
½ teaspoon bicarbonate of soda
½ teaspoon salt
1 teaspoon ground cinnamon
1 teaspoon vanilla essence
2 medium eggs, beaten

CHOCOLATE COURGETTE CAKE

for the flavouring use one or more of the following
about 115 g/4 oz chopped or puréed apple, mashed banana, raisins, walnuts, chocolate chips, coconut, apricots, or chopped fresh peaches

for the topping
60 g/2 oz brown sugar
1 teaspoon plain flour
1 teaspoon ground cinnamon

200 g/7 oz plain flour
1 teaspoon baking powder
½ teaspoon bicarbonate of soda
½ teaspoon salt
115 g/4 oz caster sugar
170 ml/6 fl oz vegetable oil
2 large eggs, beaten
225 g/8 oz courgettes (peeled weight)
170 g/6 oz plain chocolate
60 g/2 oz chopped walnuts

Mix all the ingredients together and pour into a 30 × 23 × 5 cm/ 12 × 9 × 2 inch oblong or 23 cm/9 inch round cake tin.

Mix together the topping ingredients and sprinkle over the cake. Bake in a preheated oven at 190°C/375°F/Gas 5 for 40–60 minutes. Allow to cool and store in an airtight tin.

The finished cake is also delicious, served warm with cream, as a pudding.

The courgette dissolves completely and adds moisture to this dense chocolate cake. I bake it in two 20 cm/8 inch sandwich tins and fill the sandwich with chocolate buttercream, or in a 900 g/2 lb loaf tin, when I serve it sliced with rich vanilla ice cream.

Grease and flour your chosen tins (see above) and preheat the oven to 180°C/360°F/Gas 4.

Sift all the dry ingredients into a large bowl. Beat the oil into the eggs. Finely grate the courgettes, collecting any juice. Melt the chocolate in a bowl over simmering water. Mix the egg and oil into the dry ingredients, then add the chocolate and courgettes. Stir to combine everything well, then mix in the nuts.

Either divide the batter between the two sandwich tins and bake for 25–30 minutes, or pour into the loaf tin and bake for 50–55 minutes. The cake should be well risen and pulling slightly away from the sides of the tin. Remove from the oven, leave for 5 minutes, then turn on to a wire rack to cool.

FRESH LEMON AND COCONUT CAKE

3 large eggs
weight of the eggs in soft butter,
   caster sugar and self-raising flour
grated rind of 1 large lemon
85 g/3 oz desiccated coconut
3 tablespoons milk

for the filling
juice of 1 lemon
30 g/1 oz butter
30 g/1 oz caster sugar
1 egg, beaten

for the icing
115 g/4 oz icing sugar, sifted
60 g/2 oz soft butter
60 g/2 oz desiccated coconut
1 teaspoon milk

This rich cake relies on the sharp lemon filling to offset the sweet coconut buttercream icing.

Beat the eggs. Cream the butter with the sugar until light, then add the beaten egg a little at a time, beating well after each addition. If the mixture begins to curdle, add a little flour. Fold in the remaining flour, the lemon rind and the coconut, adding the milk to give a soft dropping consistency. Divide between 2 prepared 20 cm/8 inch sandwich tins and bake in a preheated oven at 180°C/360°F/Gas 4, until well risen and golden brown. Remove from the oven and allow to cool on a rack while you prepare the filling.

In a bowl over a pan of simmering water, mix together the ingredients for the filling. Stir until the sugar has dissolved, then cook until the curd thickens, stirring often. Allow to cool and use to sandwich the two cakes together.

To ice, combine the sugar and butter. Beat in the coconut and milk to give a soft but not runny icing. Spread over the top and sides of the cake and leave for 3–4 hours to set slightly.

PARSNIP AND LEMON CAKE

285 g/10 oz plain flour
2 teaspoons baking powder
255 g/9 oz caster sugar
½ teaspoon salt
4 size 2 eggs, beaten
2 tablespoons grated lemon rind
1 tablespoon lemon juice
1 teaspoon vanilla essence
200 ml/8 fl oz vegetable oil
285 g/10 oz finely grated parsnip

for the frosting
115 g/4 oz cream cheese
225 g/8 oz icing sugar
a squeeze of lemon juice

*Parsnip gives this cake moistness
and a delicious flavour. No one
will know the secret ingredient
unless told, so you can keep your
guests guessing.*

*This cake may also be baked in
two 20 cm/8 inch sandwich tins
for 35–40 minutes and then filled
and covered with cream cheese
frosting.*

Sift together the flour, baking
powder, sugar and salt. In a large
bowl beat the eggs with the lemon
rind and juice and vanilla, then
beat in the oil. Fold in the flour
and the parsnip. Pour the batter
into a shallow greased and floured
33 × 23 cm/13 × 9 inch tin and
bake in a preheated oven at
180°C/360°F/Gas 4 for 50–60
minutes. The cake should be well
risen, golden brown and just
pulling from the sides of the tin.
Allow to cool, then slice into bars.

To make the frosting, beat the
ingredients together and use as
required.

MUESLI AND APPLE JUICE CAKE

115 g/4 oz muesli
60 g/2 oz sultanas
150 ml/¼ pint apple juice
140 g/5 oz soft margarine
140 g/5 oz caster sugar
3 size 2 eggs, beaten
225 g/8 oz self-raising flour

*This recipe comes from Gillian
Reynolds, who writes radio
reviews for* The Daily Telegraph.

Put the muesli and sultanas to soak
in the apple juice overnight. Beat
the margarine and sugar until the
mixture is light, then beat in the
eggs a little at a time.

Fold in the flour and muesli
mixture and when everything is
well combined, spoon the batter
into a greased, floured 20 cm/
8 inch cake tin. Bake in a preheated oven at 180°C/360°F/Gas 4
for 60–75 minutes, or until well
risen and golden brown. Allow to
cool, then store in an airtight tin.

COURGETTE AND CINNAMON CAKE

285 g/10 oz self-raising flour
½ teaspoon salt
1 tablespoon ground cinnamon
200 g/7 oz soft brown sugar
3 size 2 eggs, beaten
220 ml/8 fl oz vegetable oil
340 g/12 oz finely grated courgette
60 g/2 oz chopped mixed peel
60 g/2 oz chopped pecan nuts

This is delicious: a moist, densely textured cake similar to, though lighter than, carrot cake. Ice it if you like with cream cheese frosting, see next recipe. It is important that the courgettes are grated by hand.

Sift together the flour, salt and cinnamon. Mix with the sugar. Beat the eggs with the oil. Mix all the ingredients together to combine well, and pour into a greased, floured 33 × 23 × 5 cm/13 × 9 × 2 inch tin.

Bake in a preheated oven at 190°C/375°F/Gas 5 for 45–50 minutes, or until a tester inserted in the centre comes out clean. Allow to cool, then remove from the tin.

FRUIT AND NUT CARROT CAKE

170 g/6 oz plain flour
1 teaspoon baking powder
1 teaspoon bicarbonate of soda
¼ teaspoon salt
3 teaspoons mixed spice
170 ml/6 fl oz sunflower oil
3 size 2 eggs, beaten
170 g/6 oz soft brown sugar
60 g/2 oz ready-to-eat prunes, chopped
60 g/2 oz chopped walnuts
170 g/6 oz carrots (peeled weight), finely grated

for the cream cheese frosting
115 g/4 oz cream cheese
225 g/8 oz icing sugar
1 teaspoon grated lemon rind

Sift the flour, baking powder, soda, salt and spice into a large bowl, making sure they are well mixed. Whisk or blend together the oil, eggs and brown sugar until smooth. Stir this mixture with the prunes, walnuts and carrots into the flour.

Fold everything together well and pour into a 900 g/2 lb loaf tin. Bake in a preheated oven at 180°C/360°F/Gas 4 for 50–60 minutes, or until a tester inserted in the centre comes out clean.

Allow to cool before icing, if desired. To make the cream cheese frosting, beat everything together well.

SPICE CAKE
with whipped brown sugar frosting

225 g/8 oz self-raising flour
1 teaspoon cinnamon
¼ teaspoon nutmeg
1 teaspoon mixed spice
½ teaspoon ground ginger
115 g/4 oz soft margarine
170 g/6 oz caster sugar
1 size 2 egg, beaten
140 ml/¼ pint buttermilk
½ teaspoon vanilla

for the frosting
115 g/4 oz soft brown sugar
60 g/2 oz golden syrup
1 size 2 egg white
a pinch of salt
a large pinch cream of tartar
2 tablespoons water
¼ teaspoon vanilla essence

Sift the flour with the spices. Cream the margarine and sugar together and beat until light and fluffy, then add the beaten egg. Mix the buttermilk with the vanilla and fold in one third, followed by one third of the flour. Continue until everything is well combined. Spoon the batter into a greased 20 cm/8 inch cake tin and bake in a preheated oven at 180°C/360°F/Gas 4 for 60–75 minutes, or until risen and pale golden brown. Allow to cool on a rack.

To make the frosting, place all the ingredients except the vanilla in a bowl over a pan of simmering water, and beat the mixture with an electric whisk until it stands in soft peaks. Remove from the heat, add the vanilla and continue beating for 3–4 minutes. By this time the mixture should be very thick. Spread over the cake and allow to cool.

WHITE WINE CAKE

85 g/3 oz butter
140 g/5 oz caster sugar
4 egg yolks
200 g/7 oz self-raising flour
½ teaspoon baking powder
¼ teaspoon almond essence
80 ml/3 fl oz white wine

to finish
175 ml/⅓ pint whipping cream
icing sugar to taste
1–2 tablespoons almond liqueur,
  optional
seedless green grapes

If you would prefer not to use wine in this recipe, substitute the same amount of milk.

Cream the butter with the sugar and beat until light and fluffy. Beat in the yolks, one at a time. Sift the flour with the baking powder and add the essence to the wine. Fold in one third of the flour, followed by half the wine. Continue to add the ingredients until they are all used, ending with the flour.

Pour the batter into 2 greased and lined 18 cm/7 inch sandwich tins and bake in a preheated oven at 190°C/375°F/Gas 5 for 25 minutes, or until the cake is well risen, light brown and has started to shrink from the sides of the tin. Allow to cool for 5 minutes, then turn on to a rack.

When the cake is cold, fill with whipped cream, sweetened to taste and flavoured with almond liqueur and seedless grapes. Dust the top lightly with icing sugar.

COCONUT AND RASPBERRY BARS

225 g/8 oz shortcrust pastry
2–3 tablespoons raspberry jam
115 g/4 oz caster sugar
115 g/4 oz soft margarine
2 size 3 eggs
115 g/4 oz self-raising flour
60 g/2 oz desiccated coconut
1 tablespoon granulated sugar

These light coconut sponge bars disappeared in minutes when I tried out the recipe, so they must be judged a great success.

Line a shallow greased oblong cake tin, about 30 × 15 cm/ 12 × 6 inches, with the pastry. Trim the edges neatly. Spread over the jam in an even layer.

Beat together all the remaining ingredients, except the granulated sugar, and spread over the jam. Sprinkle the reserved sugar on top.

Bake in a preheated oven at 180°C/360°F/Gas 4 for 25–35 minutes or until the sponge is well risen and the pastry golden. Allow to cool before cutting into slices. Store in an airtight tin.

STEM GINGER AND LEMON BUNS

makes 12–18
115 g/4 oz soft butter
115 g/4 oz caster sugar
2 size 2 eggs, beaten
115 g/4 oz self-raising flour
½ teaspoon ground ginger
grated rind and juice of ½ lemon
2 large pieces stem ginger, finely chopped

to ice
85 g/3 oz icing sugar
juice and rind of ½ lemon
1 piece stem ginger, chopped

Use stem ginger preserved in syrup for these light spicy buns.

Cream the butter and sugar until light, then add the egg, a little at a time, beating well. Fold in the flour, ginger, lemon rind and juice, then add the ginger pieces.

Spoon the mixture into paper cases in bun tins and bake in a preheated oven at 200°C/400°F/Gas 6 for 20 minutes, until risen and golden brown. Remove from the oven and allow to cool.

To decorate, mix the icing sugar, lemon juice and rind to a thick paste (you may not need all the juice). Spread a little icing on each bun and top with a piece of ginger.

MINT CHOCOLATE CUPCAKES

makes 12
125 g/4½ oz soft margarine
125 g/4½ oz caster sugar
2 size 2 eggs, beaten
115 g/4 oz self-raising flour
30 g/1 oz cocoa powder

for the icing
45 g/1½ oz soft butter
115 g/4 oz icing sugar
green food colouring
peppermint essence

Cream the margarine with the sugar until light and fluffy, then add the egg a little at a time, beating well between each addition. Sift the flour with the cocoa powder and fold this into the egg mixture.

Line 12 deep bun tins with paper cases and divide the batter between them. Bake in a preheated oven at 180°C/360°F/Gas 4 for 15–20 minutes. Remove and allow to cool on a rack.

Make the icing by beating the butter and sugar together with a few drops of food colouring and peppermint essence to taste until light and fluffy. Cut small circles from the top of each cake. Put in a teaspoonful of icing and replace the lids.

Lamingtons

4 eggs
115 g/4 oz caster sugar
115 g/4 oz plain flour, sifted
60 g/2 oz melted butter

for the icing
285 g/10 oz icing sugar
45 g/1½ oz cocoa powder
100 ml/⅙ pint warm milk
30 g/1 oz melted butter
255 g/9 oz desiccated coconut

No one watching the amazingly popular Australian 'soaps' on television will be in any doubt that lamingtons are an essential item on the Antipodean tea table.

In the bowl of an electric mixer beat the eggs and sugar until the mixture is thick and holds a trail when the beater is lifted from it. Alternatively, beat the eggs and sugar with a hand held beater over a pan of simmering water for about 10 minutes.

When you have a dense white foam, carefully fold in the flour and then the melted butter. Pour the batter into a shallow greased and floured 30 × 18 cm/
12 × 7 inch tin. Bake in a preheated oven at 180°C/360°F/ Gas 4 for 30 minutes, until well risen and golden brown. Allow to cool on a rack.

While the cake is cooling, combine the icing sugar, cocoa, milk and butter to make a thin chocolate icing. Have the coconut ready in a wide dish.

When cold, cut the cake into 5 cm/2 inch squares and carefully dip each one into the icing and then into the coconut. Make sure all sides are well covered with the coating. Replace on the rack until set and store in an airtight tin.

LITTLE LIME TARTS

makes 18
**shortcrust pastry made with
  225 g/8 oz flour (page 71)
1 tin sweetened condensed milk
3 egg yolks
rind and juice of 3 limes**

These tangy tarts are wonderfully simple to make.

Roll out the pastry thinly, cut 8 cm/3 inch circles and use these to line shallow tart tins.

Beat together the remaining ingredients. Spoon the filling into the prepared pastry cases, filling about two-thirds full. Bake the tarts in a preheated oven at 180°C/360°F/Gas 4 for 15–20 minutes. Allow to cool, then store in an airtight tin.

ROCK BUNS

makes 15
**225 g/8 oz plain flour
pinch of salt
2 teaspoons baking powder
60 g/2 oz butter
60 g/2 oz lard
115 g/4 oz demerara sugar
115 g/4 oz mixed fruit
1 teaspoon mixed spice
grated rind of 1 lemon
1 size 3 egg, beaten with 1
  tablespoon milk**

After what was possibly my first attempt at cooking, I can remember proudly bearing rock buns home from school. Years later I tried again to make these delicious crumbly cakes after tasting the rock buns on sale at Wisley, the headquarters of the Royal Horticultural Society, in their excellent tea room.

Sift the flour, salt and baking powder and rub in the fats. I use a food processor for this stage, then tip the crumbs into a large bowl.

Toss the sugar, fruit, spice and lemon rind into the mixture, then form a stiff dough with the egg. The mixture should just hold together. Place a large spoonful of the mixture on a greased baking sheet, keeping a rocky appearance.

Bake in a preheated oven at 200°C/400°F/Gas 6 for 15–20 minutes, until golden brown.

LITTLE CURD CHEESE TARTS

makes 18
225 g/8 oz shortcrust pastry (page 71)
raspberry jam
115 g/4 oz curd cheese
85 g/3 oz caster sugar
2 egg yolks
grated rind of ½ lemon
a squeeze of lemon juice
85 g/3 oz ground almonds
a few slivered almonds to decorate

These little cheese tarts are similar to the 'Maids of honour' traditionally associated with Henry VIII. I like to put a very small spoonful of raspberry jam in each tart case before adding the cheese mixture.

Line 18 bun tins with pastry and put a little jam in each one. Beat the cheese, sugar and egg yolks together until smooth. Add the remaining ingredients and mix well. Divide this mixture between the tartlets and sprinkle on a few slivered almonds.

Bake in a preheated oven at 180°C/360°F/Gas 4 for about 20 minutes, until the pastry is cooked and the tops of the buns are lightly browned.

ALMOND AND LEMON BUNS

makes 12–18
140 g/5 oz soft butter
140 g/5 oz caster sugar
2 size 2 eggs, beaten
115 g/4 oz self-raising flour
30 g/1 oz ground almonds
juice and rind of ½ lemon

for the icing
115 g/4 oz icing sugar
1–2 tablespoons lemon juice

to decorate
slivered almonds

Cream the butter and sugar until light and fluffy. Beat in the egg a little at a time, adding a teaspoon of flour if the mixture begins to curdle. Fold in the remaining ingredients and divide between 12–18 paper cake cases.

Bake in a preheated oven at 180°C/360°F/Gas 4 for 20 minutes, or until the cakes are well risen and golden brown.

Allow to cool. Mix the sugar with the lemon juice, ice the buns, and decorate with a few slivered almonds.

CRUMBLY COCONUT AND CHOCOLATE SQUARES

170 g/6 oz soft butter
115 g/4 oz soft light brown sugar
3 eggs, separated
1 teaspoon vanilla essence
225 g/8 oz selfraising flour
¼ teaspoon salt
225 g/8 oz cooking chocolate drops
170 g/6 oz sweetened desiccated coconut
170 g/6 oz soft brown sugar for the meringue

Originating in the US, these chewy crumbly squares are a cross between a biscuit and a cake. They are impossible to cut tidily, very rich, and absolutely delicious.

Mix together butter, sugar, egg yolks and vanilla until well blended. Add the flour and salt and stir until you have a smooth soft dough. Spread this over the base of a greased 33 × 23 × 5 cm/13 × 9 × 2 inch tin. Sprinkle over the chocolate drops and coconut in an even layer.

For the meringue, beat the egg whites until stiff, then beat in the brown sugar. Continue to beat until the mixture is stiff and glossy. Spread this carefully over the layer of chocolate and coconut – this is quite fiddly as the filling has a tendency to move as you spread.

Bake the cake in a preheated oven at 180°C/360°F/Gas 4 for 35–40 minutes. The meringue will have risen, set and started to crack. Allow to cool, then slice into small squares.

WALNUT, SESAME AND OATMEAL BARS

140 g/5 oz shortcrust pastry (page 71)
115 g/4 oz butter
115 g/4 oz light muscovado sugar
1 tablespoon golden syrup
60 g/2 oz chopped walnuts
85 g/3 oz porridge oats
30 g/1 oz sesame seeds

Something like a cross between a flapjack and a treacle tart, these deliciously rich bars are packed with nuts, oats, brown sugar and calories.

Line a shallow 18 cm/7 inch square tin with the pastry.

Warm the butter, sugar and syrup in a saucepan and stir well. Add the nuts, oats and sesame seeds and give everything another good stir. Pour this mixture into the pastry shell and bake in a preheated oven at 200°C/400°F/ Gas 6 for 25–30 minutes, until the pastry and filling are a golden brown. Allow to cool in the tin, then cut into slices.

FRUIT AND NUT SLICES

170 g/6 oz mixed raisins, currants and sultanas
170 g/6 oz roughly chopped mixed nuts
415 ml/¾ pint apple juice
225 g/8 oz wholemeal flour
1 teaspoon baking powder
85 g/3 oz soft brown sugar
1 size 2 egg, beaten

for the topping
2–3 tablespoons apple and pear spread (from health food stores)

Containing only natural ingredients, these slices could almost be said to be good for you.

Put the fruit, nuts and apple juice into a bowl and leave overnight.

Mix together the remaining ingredients and pour into a shallow 30 × 15 cm/12 × 6 inch tin. Bake in a preheated oven at 190°C/375°F/Gas 5 for 40–45 minutes.

Spread the apple topping on while the cake is still warm, allow to cool, then slice into bars.

CHEWY DATE AND COCONUT BARS

115 g/4 oz margarine
1 large tablespoon golden syrup
1 size 2 egg, beaten
140 g/5 oz chopped dates
170 g/6 oz demerara sugar
85 g/3 oz desiccated coconut
115 g/4 oz self-raising flour

My sister Maureen gave me this recipe. It is simplicity itself to make and delicious to eat. The mixture rises during cooking but then sinks down to give a chewy, wickedly sweet cross between a cake and a biscuit.

Melt the margarine and syrup together. Allow them to cool for 5 minutes, then beat in the egg. Mix all the dry ingredients together, then add the egg mixture and stir well. Tip the mixture into an 18 cm/7 inch square tin and press it down evenly.

Bake in a preheated oven at 160°C/325°F/Gas 3 for 30 minutes or until risen and golden brown. The cake will still be a little soft in the centre. Allow to cool, then slice into bars.

RAISIN AND COCONUT BARS

225 g/8 oz muscatel raisins
275 ml/½ pint orange juice
340 g/12 oz plain flour
225 g/8 oz soft brown sugar
½ teaspoon salt
340 g/12 oz block margarine or
    butter
115 g/4 oz desiccated coconut
115 g/4 oz medium oats

I have tried cutting down on the butter in these delicious raisin bars, but you really do need the full amount.

Place the raisins with the orange juice in a saucepan and bring the mixture to the boil. Simmer for 20–25 minutes until the fruit is soft and the mixture thick, like jam.

Mix the flour, sugar and salt and rub in the butter. When this resembles coarse breadcrumbs, add the coconut and oats. Spread half the mixture over the base of a 33 × 23 × 5 cm/13 × 9 × 2 inch tin and press down lightly. Spread the raisin 'jam' over the base, then cover with the remaining crumbs, pressing down.

Bake in a preheated oven at 180°C/360°F/Gas 4 for 40–45 minutes, or until the top is light golden brown. Remove and allow to cool, then cut into bars.

APPLE AND RAISIN SPICE BARS

3 medium cooking apples
115 g/4 oz softened butter
170 g/6 oz soft brown sugar
1 large egg, beaten
½ teaspoon vanilla essence
225 g/8 oz plain flour
2 teaspoons ground cinnamon
½ teaspoon ground nutmeg
½ teaspoon salt
½ teaspoon baking powder
1 teaspoon bicarbonate of soda
115 g/4 oz raisins

This apple cake becomes stickier and its spicy flavour develops if it is kept in an airtight tin for 48 hours.

Peel, core and chop the apples. Cook them with a very little water until soft and pulpy, to make about 275 ml/½ pint thick apple purée.

Beat the butter and sugar together, add the egg and vanilla, then stir in the apple. Have the flour ready sifted with the remaining dry ingredients and fold this in along with the raisins.

Pour the mixture into a shallow greased 30 × 18 cm/12 × 7 inch tin and bake in a preheated oven at 190°C/375°F/Gas 5 for 30–40 minutes, until well risen and springy when touched in the centre. Remove from the oven and allow to cool, then slice into bars. Store in an airtight tin.

WHITE CHOCOLATE CAKE
with dark chocolate chips

115 g/4 oz butter
170 g/6 oz white chocolate
4 size 2 eggs
1 teaspoon vanilla essence
115 g/4 oz caster sugar
200 g/7 oz plain flour
1 teaspoon baking powder
¼ teaspoon salt
115 g/4 oz plain chocolate chips

This cake is very rich, so slice it into small squares.

Melt the butter with the white chocolate and allow to cool slightly. Beat in the eggs, vanilla and sugar, mixing until well combined. Now fold in the flour, baking powder, salt and chocolate chips. Mix until everything is just moistened, then pour the batter into a shallow greased 33 × 23 cm/ 13 × 9 inch tin.

Bake in a preheated oven at 180°C/360°F/Gas 4 for 20 minutes. The cake will be only just cooked in the centre. Allow to cool, then slice into bars.

OAT CHOCOLATE BROWNIE

for the base
225 g/8 oz porridge oats
85 g/3 oz plain flour
170 g/6 oz soft brown sugar
170 g/6 oz melted butter
½ teaspoon bicarbonate of soda

for the top
9 tablespoons cocoa powder
3 tablespoons vegetable oil
400 g/14 oz caster sugar
4 size 2 eggs, beaten
1 teaspoon vanilla essence
170 g/6 oz plain flour
1 teaspoon baking powder
1 teaspoon salt

This is a very rich, sticky brownie, so cut small slices and store the remainder in an airtight tin.

Mix together all the ingredients for the base and press three quarters of the crumbs into a 33 × 23 × 5 cm/13 × 9 × 2 inch tin. Bake in a preheated oven at 180°C/360°C/ Gas 4 for 10 minutes.

Mix together all the ingredients for the top until well blended, and pour the batter over the cooled oat base. Sprinkle the reserved oat mixture over the top and return to the oven for 30–40 minutes. Don't overbake, as the finished cake should be soft and moist. Cut into bars when cold.

DOUBLE CHOCOLATE MINT BROWNIE

200 g/7 oz plain flour
1 teaspoon baking powder
60 g/2 oz cocoa powder
½ teaspoon salt
225 g/8 oz soft margarine
285 g/10 oz caster sugar
4 size 3 eggs
1 teaspoon vanilla essence
60 g/2 oz chopped walnuts

for the icing
225 g/8 oz icing sugar
60 g/2 oz soft butter
milk to mix
peppermint essence

to finish
115 g/4 oz plain chocolate

This extravagant brownie satisfies my cravings as a chocaholic. Try to find vanilla and peppermint essences rather than flavourings as the taste is far superior.

Sift together the flour, baking powder, cocoa and salt. Cream the margarine with the caster sugar until fluffy, then beat in the eggs and vanilla essence, adding a little flour if the mixture starts to curdle. Fold in the rest of the flour and the walnuts. Pour the mixture into a greased 33 × 23 × 5 cm/13 × 9 × 2 inch tin.

Bake in a preheated oven at 180°C/360°F/Gas 4 for 25–30 minutes. The cake will be slightly undercooked and may sink a little in the middle. Allow to cool.

Make buttercream icing by combining the ingredients, and flavour with peppermint essence to taste. Spread this over the cooled cake. When set, melt the chocolate in a bowl over simmering water and spread over the peppermint icing. Cut into small pieces to serve.

PALMIERS

225 g/8 oz puff pastry
caster sugar
plain chocolate to decorate

These pastries are so called because they are shaped like palm leaves and traditionally eaten in France on Palm Sunday.

Sprinkle a pastry board generously with sugar and roll out the pastry. Turn the dough over and again, cover with sugar and roll it in well. When you have a strip about 30 × 12 cm/12 × 5 inches, place the dough short side facing you and turn the sides in once, then again to meet in the middle. Fold one side on to the other and press down well.

Slice the roll thinly into hearts, place on a well greased baking sheet, and bake in a preheated oven at 220°C/425°F/Gas 7 for 8 minutes. Turn the hearts and cook until both sides are golden brown. Allow to cool on a rack.

To decorate, melt a little chocolate in a bowl over simmering water, and dip the tip of the hearts in to coat. Allow to set.

YORKSHIRE PARKIN

60 g/2 oz butter
60 g/2 oz lard
115 g/4 oz soft brown sugar
115 g/4 oz golden syrup
115 g/4 oz black treacle
1 egg, beaten
140 ml/¼ pint milk
225 g/8 oz medium oatmeal
225 g/8 oz plain flour
1 heaped teaspoon ground ginger
½ teaspoon salt
1 teaspoon bicarbonate soda

Yorkshire parkin is a traditional bonfire night cake, robust in both texture and flavour. It is the perfect cake to eat on a cold night outdoors.

Melt the butter, lard, sugar, syrup and treacle over a low heat. Add the egg with half the milk. Put the oatmeal, flour, ginger and salt into a large bowl and pour in the treacle mixture. Mix everything together well. Stir the bicarbonate of soda into the remaining milk and mix this in too. Pour the mixture into a shallow well buttered 27 × 23 cm/11 × 9 inch tin and bake in the centre of a preheated oven at 190°C/375°F/ Gas 5 for 35–45 minutes. Allow to cool, then cut into squares and store in an airtight tin for 2–3 days before eating.

CHAPTER 2

Breakfast
&
teatime treats

THE RECIPES IN this chapter have baking powder as the raising agent, which means home baked goodness in minutes. If you've never considered freshly baked American muffins for breakfast, now is the time to revolutionize your morning routine – at least at weekends! Then there are scones, Scotch pancakes, Welsh cakes, banana bread and French toast, all equally delightful for brunch or a lazy tea by the fire. Just add butter, and relax.

A selection of biscuits begins on page 48. The word 'biscuit' comes from the French, meaning twice cooked (for extra crispness), but nowadays we manage it in one go. Freshly made biscuits still warm from the oven are now on offer at many high street bakers. However, the homemade variety tastes better as well as being cheaper, so put away your purse and get out the mixing bowl.

Don't forget to allow biscuits to cool on a rack, and then store in an airtight tin to keep them tasting fresh and crisp.

DATE AND WALNUT MUFFINS

makes 12–18
115 g/4 oz plain flour
85 g/3 oz wholemeal flour
30 g/1 oz wheatgerm
1 level tablespoon baking powder
½ teaspoon salt
115 g/4 oz soft brown sugar
115 g/4 oz chopped stoned dates
60 g/2 oz chopped walnuts
2 eggs, beaten
175 ml/⅓ pint milk
100 ml/⅙ pint corn oil

American muffins can be freshly baked for breakfast.

Line your deepest bun tins with paper cases and heat the oven to 180°C/360°F/Gas 4. In a deep bowl mix the flours, wheatgerm, salt and baking powder well, then add the sugar, dates and walnuts.

In another bowl beat together the eggs, milk and oil. Add the wet ingredients to the dry, stirring until just combined. Spoon the mixture into the paper cases and bake for 20 minutes, until well risen and golden brown.

Serve warm, split and buttered.

CRANBERRY WHOLEWHEAT MUFFINS

makes 12–18
115 g/4 oz butter
115 g/4 oz caster sugar
2 large eggs
220 ml/8 fl oz milk
115 g/4 oz plain flour
115 g/4 oz wholemeal flour
1 tablespoon baking powder
60 g/2 oz chopped walnuts
115 g/4 oz cranberries

Cream together the butter and sugar and beat in the eggs. Add the milk and then the flours, baking powder, nuts and berries. Mix until the ingredients are moistened, but do not beat. Put the mixture into 12–18 deep mince pie or bun tins lined with paper cases, filling them to the top, and bake in a preheated oven at 180°C/360°F/Gas 4 for 30–35 minutes, until well risen and golden brown. Serve warm with butter.

MOLASSES BRAN MUFFINS

makes 12–18
60 g/2 oz soft margarine
85 g/3 oz light muscovado sugar
2 tablespoons black treacle
2 size 3 eggs
220 ml/8 fl oz milk
70 g/2½ oz natural bran
170 g/6 oz plain flour
1½ teaspoons baking powder
½ teaspoon bicarbonate of soda
¾ teaspoon salt
85 g/3 oz raisins

This recipe comes from Mrs F. Horsburgh, who lives in Exmouth, Devon. The muffins are very light and airy.

Cream the margarine and beat in the treacle. Add the eggs one at a time, mixing well. Stir in the milk and then the bran, beating until combined. Sift the flour, baking powder, bicarbonate of soda and salt together and fold thoroughly into the bran mixture. Add the raisins.

Spoon the mixture into paper cases in deep bun tins and bake in a preheated oven at 200°C/400°F/Gas 6 for 15–20 minutes, until well risen and a deep brown.

Serve warm, split open with a knob of butter.

BLACKBERRY AND CORNMEAL MUFFINS

makes 12–18
200 g/7 oz plain flour
115 g/4 oz caster sugar
½ teaspoon salt
30 g/1 oz cornmeal (polenta)
1 tablespoon baking powder
60 g/2 oz sunflower seeds, optional
2 size 2 eggs
115 g/4 oz melted butter
220 ml/8 fl oz buttermilk, or milk soured with lemon juice (page 41)
115 g/4 oz frozen blackberries

When they are available, try fresh blueberries in this recipe.

Sift the flour, sugar, salt, cornmeal and baking powder together into a large bowl. Add the sunflower seeds. Beat the eggs with the butter and buttermilk and stir in until the mixture is just mixed. Fold in the blackberries, keeping the ripples of colour the juice makes, then spoon the mixture into lined bun tins, filling three-quarters full.

Bake in a preheated oven at 180°C/360°F/Gas 4 for 25–30 minutes. Serve warm, split and buttered.

ORANGE AND DATE WHOLEWHEAT MUFFINS

makes 12–18
115 g/4 oz plain flour
115 g/4 oz wholemeal flour
115 g/4 oz muscovado sugar
2 teaspoons baking powder
½ teaspoon salt
1 medium orange
1 size 3 egg
3 tablespoons sunflower oil
220 ml/8 fl oz buttermilk or milk soured with lemon juice, see below
60 g/2 oz stoned, chopped dates

These American breakfast muffins are so quick and easy to make. For the very best results choose a thin skinned orange, use your deepest bun tins and don't overmix the batter.

If you can't find buttermilk at your local supermarket, use milk soured with a teaspoon of lemon juice and allowed to stand at room temperature for 15 minutes.

Line the bun tins with paper cases. Sift all the dry ingredients into a large bowl, tipping in any bran that collects in the sieve. Scrub the orange well to remove any wax, then cut into quarters and take out the pips. Put the orange into a food processor or blender and process until it is finely chopped. Add the egg, sunflower oil and milk and continue to process until everything is well mixed.

Pour this mixture on to the dry ingredients, add the dates and stir until the mixture is just combined. The mixture will be lumpy. Spoon the batter into the paper cases, filling them about ¾ full, and bake the muffins in a preheated oven at 200°C/400°F/Gas 6 for 20–25 minutes. Serve warm, split open, with a knob of butter.

BANANA BREAD

3–4 ripe medium bananas, mashed
3 medium eggs, beaten
1 teaspoon vanilla
190 ml/7 fl oz sunflower oil
125 g/4½ oz wholemeal flour
125 g/4½ oz plain flour
2 teaspoons baking powder
¼ teaspoon salt
115 g/4 oz soft brown sugar
60 g/2 oz chopped walnuts,
   optional

The perfect way to use up three or four overripe bananas is in this tea bread. Made with baking powder and oil instead of butter, it is very quick to put together.

Mix the bananas, eggs, vanilla and oil, beating them well together. Sift the flours with the baking powder and salt, adding any bran that is left in the sieve. Put the sugar into the dry ingredients, then add them to the wet ingredients and mix well. Stir in the nuts.

Pour the mixture into a greased 900 g/2 lb loaf tin and bake in a preheated oven at 160°C/325°F/Gas 3 for 55–65 minutes. The bread should be risen and brown, and a tester inserted in the middle should come out clean.

Allow to cool on a rack and serve sliced and buttered.

PUMPKIN BREAD

115 g/4 oz softened butter
170 g/6 oz caster sugar
2 small eggs, beaten
420 ml/¾ pint pumpkin purée
225 g/8 oz plain flour
½ teaspoon bicarbonate of soda
1½ teaspoons baking powder
½ teaspoon salt
2 teaspoons mixed spice
1 teaspoon ground cinnamon
115 g/4 oz walnuts

Once Halloween has passed don't throw the pumpkin away. Try making pumpkin bread, a moist loaf raised with baking powder that can be served plain or buttered for tea.

The pumpkin purée must be dry and thick. Make it by steaming 450 g/1 lb pumpkin or by cooking in a microwave with 2 tablespoons water.

Cream the butter with the sugar and add the eggs. Stir in the pumpkin, then fold in the flour, sifted with the other dry ingredients. Fold in the nuts and pour into a greased loaf tin.

Bake in a preheated oven at 160°C/325°F/Gas 3 for 75–90 minutes. The cake is cooked when a tester inserted in the centre comes out clean.

FRUIT AND NUT TEA BREAD

170 g/6 oz mixed fruit (raisins, dates, sultanas, prunes)
170 ml/6 fl oz hot tea
1 size 3 egg, beaten
1 tablespoon melted butter
1 teaspoon vanilla essence
170 g/6 oz plain flour
60 g/2 oz light muscovado sugar
1 rounded teaspoon baking powder
60 g/2 oz chopped walnuts

Best made the day before eating, this fruit and nut tea bread becomes soft and moist when stored, well wrapped, overnight.

If you use dates or prunes chop them small. Soak the fruit in the hot tea for 1 hour. Beat the egg with the butter and vanilla. Sift the flour into a large bowl and stir in the sugar. Mix the baking powder into the fruit, add the egg mixture, and stir well. Pour the frothing mixture on to the flour, add the nuts and stir until combined.

Pour the batter into a greased, floured 450 g/1 lb loaf tin and bake in a preheated oven at 160°C/325°F/Gas 3 for 55–60 minutes, or until a tester inserted in the centre comes out clean.

Allow to cool on a rack and store tightly wrapped in foil overnight. Serve thinly sliced with butter.

FRENCH TOAST

2 eggs, beaten
175 ml/⅓ pint creamy milk
6–8 slices two-day-old white or French bread
butter for frying

I like French toast with maple syrup and crisp bacon, but you can add cinnamon sugar, golden syrup, chocolate spread or honey.

Mix the eggs with the milk and soak the bread slices for 2–3 minutes. Heat the butter in a pan and fry the soaked bread, a few slices at a time, until golden brown on each side. Keep hot while you fry the rest.

CINNAMON TOAST

2 slices hot well-buttered toast per person
85 g/3 oz caster sugar
2–3 teaspoons cinnamon

Mix the sugar and spice and sprinkle over the hot buttered toast.

SCOTCH PANCAKES

115 g/4 oz plain flour
½ teaspoon bicarbonate of soda
1 teaspoon cream of tartar
30 g/1 oz caster sugar
1 size 2 egg, beaten
140 ml/¼ pint milk

You can vary this recipe by adding a small eating apple, finely chopped, with a generous spoonful of cinnamon sugar. Or you can omit the sugar and add a dessertspoonful of golden syrup and 60 g/2 oz sultanas.

Put the dry ingredients into a bowl, make a well in the centre, and beat in the egg and milk.

Heat a griddle or heavy frying pan and brush the base with oil. Drop the batter on to the hot pan a dessertspoonful at a time. When you see bubbles rising to the surface, flip the pancakes over with a palette knife and cook the other side. Serve with lashings of butter.

FIFTEEN-MINUTE SCONES

makes 8–10
255 g/9 oz plain flour
2 level teaspoons baking powder
¼ teaspoon salt
5 tablespoons corn oil
140 ml/¼ pint milk

To make cheese scones, add 85 g/3 oz grated mature Cheddar cheese to the dry ingredients, cut the scones and brush the tops with milk, then sprinkle over a further 30 g/1 oz cheese. Serve split and filled with curd cheese and alfalfa sprouts.

Sift the dry ingredients into a bowl. Add the oil and milk and mix until you have a smooth dough. Turn out on to a floured board and knead lightly. Press or roll to 2 cm/¾-inch thick and cut scones with a 5 cm/2 inch cutter, re-rolling the trimmings.

Place the scones on a baking tray and cook in a preheated oven at 230°C/450°F/Gas 8 for 10–15 minutes, until well risen and golden brown.

QUICK AND EASY TRADITIONAL SCONES

makes 7–8
225 g/8 oz plain flour
2 teaspoons baking powder
½ teaspoon salt
60 g/2 oz butter or block margarine
140 ml/¼ pint milk

for the flavouring
60 g/2 oz raisins
½ teaspoon cinnamon
30 g/1 oz caster sugar
or
60 g/2 oz strong Cheddar cheese, grated
½ teaspoon dried herbs
¼ teaspoon mustard powder
or
60 g/2 oz chopped dates
30 g/1 oz caster sugar
grated rind of 1 orange

Feather-light homemade scones can be made more interesting by adding a variety of different flavourings as suggested here.

The secret of well risen scones is to get them into the hot oven as quickly as possible once the liquid has been added. I don't knead the dough, just mix it well, turn it out on to a floured board, pat it into shape and cut it with a knife to give asymmetrical but light and easy scones.

Sift the flour with the baking powder and salt and rub in the fat. Stir in the chosen flavouring, then the milk.

Mix well and turn out on to a floured board. Knead very lightly and pat into shape, flattening the dough to about 2.5 cm/1 inch thick. Cut 7–8 scones with a knife or a cutter, brush the tops with milk, and bake in a preheated oven at 220°C/425°F/Gas 7 for 10–15 minutes. Allow to cool and serve split with butter.

WELSH CAKES

makes 8–10
60 g/2 oz butter
60 g/2 oz lard
225 g/8 oz self-raising flour
85 g/3 oz caster sugar
½ teaspoon nutmeg
85 g/3 oz currants
1 size 2 egg
milk to mix

These traditional teatime treats are best served hot from the pan spread with good Welsh butter.

Rub the fats into the flour, then add the sugar, spice and currants. Make a soft but manageable dough with the egg and about 1 tablespoon milk if necessary. Roll out the dough to a thickness of about 2 cm/¾ inch, and cut out 8 cm/3 inch scones, re-rolling the trimmings as necessary.

Heat a nonstick frying pan over a medium heat and cook the cakes for 4–5 minutes each side, making sure they cook through without burning. This takes a little practice, but these cakes are delicious even if slightly singed.

GIRDLE SCONES

makes about 10
225 g/8 oz plain flour
1 teaspoon baking powder
60 g/2 oz butter
60 g/2 oz caster sugar
60 g/2 oz currants
1 egg, beaten
milk to mix
oil for the girdle or griddle

In Scotland a 'girdle' is a griddle, a traditional flat heavy pan heated on the cooking range.

The tricky part of this recipe is in getting the griddle heated correctly. I have found that preheating for 5 minutes over a medium gas is plenty. I then turn the gas right down when cooking the scones.

Electric plates may take longer to heat the griddle. A heavy based frying pan could be used instead.

Sift together the flour and baking powder and rub in the fat. Stir in the sugar and fruit and add the egg.

Using about 5 tablespoons milk, make a soft but manageable dough. Knead lightly and roll out to 1 cm/½ inch thick. Cut circles or wedge shaped scones and cook on a greased, preheated griddle, a few at a time, for about 5 minutes on each side, turning several times. They should be a golden brown and cooked through.

Serve at once, split and buttered.

Scottish oatcakes

makes about 20
115 g/4 oz fine oatmeal
¼ teaspoon salt
15 g/½ oz lard
about 4 tablespoons boiling water

Regular porridge oats can be ground using the metal blade of a food processor.

Oatcakes may also be cooked on top of the stove on a griddle over a medium heat. If cooked this way they should not be turned.

Pour the oats, salt and fat into a food processor and mix for 60 seconds. Add the boiling water and continue to process for a further 90 seconds. Turn the paste out on to a lightly floured board and knead lightly. While the dough is still warm, roll out to 2 mm/ ⅛ inch thick and cut into rounds or triangles.

Bake in a preheated oven at 160°C/325°F/Gas 3 for 15 minutes, until crisp but only lightly coloured.

Serve warm with preserves or cheese.

Soured cream corn bread

115 g/4 oz plain flour
115 g/4 oz cornmeal (polenta)
1 tablespoon baking powder
½ teaspoon salt
2 eggs
225 g/8 oz sweetcorn kernels (tinned)
140 ml/5 fl oz soured cream
110 ml/4 fl oz corn oil

This bread is good with spicy scrambled eggs and corned beef hash at an American brunch.

Preheat the oven to 200°C/400°F/ Gas 6. Mix the dry ingredients in a large bowl. In a food processor or blender beat the eggs, add the sweetcorn and blend for a few seconds to chop. Add the soured cream and the oil, blending to mix well. Pour this mixture over the flour and stir quickly but thoroughly.

Pour into a well greased 900 g/2 lb loaf tin and bake for 30–40 minutes, until risen and golden brown.

Serve warm, cut into thick slices, with butter.

AMERICAN TOLL HOUSE COOKIES

225 g/8 oz butter
170 g/6 oz soft brown sugar
1 teaspoon vanilla
1 egg, beaten
200 g/7 oz plain flour
½ teaspoon baking powder
¼ teaspoon salt
170 g/6 oz dark chocolate chips
115 g/4 oz chopped walnuts

I have a real weakness for these biscuits warm from the oven, but they keep well if hidden on the top shelf in an airtight tin.

Cream the butter with the sugar and vanilla until light and fluffy. Beat in the egg and fold in the flour, baking powder and salt. Then mix in the nuts and chocolate chips.

Drop teaspoons of the mixture on to a greased baking sheet about 5 cm/2 inches apart, and bake in a preheated oven at 190°C/375°F/Gas 5 for 10–12 minutes, until medium brown. Don't overcook, as they will harden when cold.

Remove the biscuits carefully to a rack and allow to cool, then store in an airtight tin.

CHOCOLATE CRUNCH BISCUITS

225 g/8 oz margarine
170 g/6 oz soft brown sugar
½ teaspoon vanilla
285 g/10 oz plain flour
½ teaspoon baking powder
a pinch of salt
2 tablespoons cocoa powder

to finish
chopped nuts or Smarties, optional

These simple crunchy biscuits are often made for friends by my daughter Jade.

Cream together the margarine, sugar and vanilla. Sift the flour with the baking powder, salt and cocoa and mix these in to form a soft dough.

Break off walnut sized pieces and roll into balls. Place on a greased baking sheet and press down slightly with a fork. You can press in a few chopped nuts or Smarties if you like. Bake in a preheated oven at 180°C/360°F/Gas 4 for 15–20 minutes. Allow to cool on a rack and store in an airtight tin when cold.

ANZAC BISCUITS

115 g/4 oz plain flour
85 g/3 oz porridge oats
85 g/3 oz desiccated coconut
170 g/6 oz caster sugar
115 g/4 oz butter
2 tablespoons golden syrup
1½ teaspoons bicarbonate of soda
2 tablespoons boiling water

Anzac biscuits hail from the Antipodes. They are named after the Australian and New Zealand Army Corps and eaten on Anzac Day, a public holiday commemorating the Anzac landing at Gallipoli in 1915.

Mix together the flour, oats, coconut and sugar. Melt the butter with the syrup. Stir the bicarbonate of soda into the boiling water and as soon as it has frothed up, mix thoroughly into the syrup. Pour this into the dry ingredients and stir well.

Drop dessertspoonfuls on to a greased baking sheet, well spaced, and bake in a preheated oven at 160°C/325°F/Gas 3 for 15–20 minutes, until golden brown.

Allow to cool. When cold store in an airtight tin.

COCONUT AND LEMON CRUNCHY BISCUITS

115 g/4 oz soft margarine
115 g/4 oz caster sugar
1 teaspoon grated lemon rind
1 teaspoon lemon juice
1 size 2 egg, beaten
170 g/6 oz plain flour
60 g/2 oz desiccated coconut

Pipe these biscuits into zigzag fingers with a plain nozzle.

Cream the margarine, sugar, lemon rind and juice until light and fluffy. Add the beaten egg, then the flour and coconut.

Spoon the mixture into a piping bag fitted with a 1 cm/½ inch plain nozzle and pipe zigzag finger biscuits about 5 cm/2 inches long on to greased baking sheets.

Bake in a preheated oven at 200°C/400°F/Gas 6 for 10–15 minutes, until light golden brown. Allow to cool on a wire rack, then store in an airtight tin.

MELTING MOMENTS

makes 24
140 g/5 oz soft margarine
115 g/4 oz caster sugar
1 egg yolk
¼ teaspoon vanilla essence
200 g/7 oz self-raising flour
30 g/1 oz cornflakes, crushed

These biscuits really do melt in your mouth and are deliciously light.

Cream the fat and sugar until light and fluffy. Add the egg yolk and vanilla and beat until combined. Mix in the flour to a stiffish dough.

Take pieces of dough about the size of a small walnut and roll into balls. Press these into the cornflake crumbs until covered on both sides. You will have about 24 round flat biscuits about 4 cm/1½ inches across. Place these, well spaced, on a baking sheet and cook in a preheated oven at 200°C/400°F/Gas 6 for 15–20 minutes.

Allow to cool for a few moments, then remove to a rack. When cold store in an airtight tin.

CUSTARD CREAM BISCUITS

makes 16
140 g/5 oz plain flour
30 g/1 oz custard powder
1 teaspoon baking powder
85 g/3 oz caster sugar
115 g/4 oz butter
1 egg, beaten

for the filling
30 g/1 oz soft butter
60 g/2 oz icing sugar

These custard creams are an easily made favourite.

Sift together flour, custard powder and baking powder, add the sugar, then rub in the butter. Add the beaten egg and stir to give a soft dough. Either form into small balls, place on a baking sheet and flatten with a fork, or pipe 2.5 cm/1 inch stars on to the baking sheet.

Cook in a preheated oven at 200°C/400°F/Gas 6 for 10 minutes, or until light brown at the edges. Remove from the tray and place on a rack until cold.

For the filling, combine the ingredients to make a butter cream icing and use it to sandwich the biscuits together.

PEANUT BUTTER COOKIES

115 g/4 oz margarine
115 g/4 oz crunchy peanut butter
115 g/4 oz soft brown sugar
1 egg, beaten
85 g/3 oz plain flour
85 g/3 oz wholemeal flour
¼ teaspoon salt

Cream together the margarine, peanut butter and sugar, add the egg and stir in the remaining ingredients. Flatten walnut sized balls on to a baking sheet with the prongs of a fork. Bake in a preheated oven at 200°C/400°F/ Gas 6 for 10–15 minutes until golden.

CINNAMON MUESLI BISCUITS

115 g/4 oz margarine
85 g/3 oz golden syrup
115 g/4 oz wholemeal flour
1½ teaspoons baking powder
115 g/4 oz muesli
1–2 teaspoons cinnamon

Cream the margarine with the syrup and mix in the dry ingredients. Drop teaspoonfuls on to a baking sheet and flatten slightly. Bake in a preheated oven at 160°C/325°F/Gas 3 for 15–20 minutes, until golden brown.

GINGER BISCUITS

115 g/4 oz plain flour
2 teaspoons granulated sugar
1 teaspoon bicarbonate of soda
1 teaspoon mixed spice
1 teaspoon ginger
60 g/2 oz golden syrup
60 g/butter, melted

Mix the dry ingredients together thoroughly. Add the syrup and butter and stir until the dough is well mixed. Break off walnut sized pieces and roll into balls. Flatten these on to a baking sheet and bake at 160°C/325°F/Gas 3 for 10–15 minutes until golden.

HAZELNUT BISCUITS

115 g/4 oz butter
225 g/8 oz plain flour
115 g/4 oz caster sugar
60 g/2 oz ground hazelnuts
1 size 2 egg, beaten
chopped hazelnuts and sugar to
finish

These delicately flavoured biscuits are delicious eaten with a cup of China tea.

Rub the butter into the flour, sugar and nuts until the mixture resembles fine crumbs. Add the egg and form the mixture into a ball of dough. Chill in the fridge for 30 minutes.

Heat the oven to 190°C/375°F/ Gas 5. Roll out the dough on a lightly floured board to about 5 mm/¼ inch thick, and cut out 8 cm/3 inch biscuits with a circular cutter. Place on a greased baking sheet and press a few pieces of hazelnut into the surface of each biscuit, then sprinkle lightly with sugar.

Bake for 15–20 minutes, until beginning to brown around the edges. Allow to cool on a rack, then store in an airtight tin.

CHAPTER
3

Yeast cookery

Iɴ ᴛʜᴇ ᴅᴀʏs before commercial bakeries, two days a week were set aside to bake bread at home. But with the rise of the large bakery came a type of bread that bears scant resemblance to the homebaked loaf. To commercial bakers lightness is all, and they offer soft white bread puffed up with chemicals. Because it doesn't need to prove, it never develops the wonderful taste and texture of the bread made at home or by small master bakers.

Recent years have seen a rebellion against this type of product, which scarcely merits the name of bread, and now supermarkets produce sliced bread made with stoneground flour and enriched with malted wheat grains.

However, not even the best supermarket bread can match the real thing baked in your own oven.

Cooking with yeast is much easier than you might at first imagine, and once you have mastered the techniques you can make an infinite variety of doughs that will fill your house with that most appetising of aromas: freshly baked bread.

You will find more festive bread recipes in the chapter beginning on page 89.

Here are some points to bear in mind when cooking with yeast.

□ Use the correct quantity of yeast. The action of yeast is inhibited by the addition of sugar, salt, butter and eggs, so larger quantities of yeast are needed for enriched doughs.

□ The dough must be moist enough to allow the yeast to act. This is especially important when using easy blend or instant yeast. Too much water in the dough will give a stodgy loaf.

Learn to feel when the dough is the right consistency: it should be soft enough to knead easily, but not sticky unless stated in the recipe. When handling moist doughs, i.e. those for brioche or Continental breads, add only enough flour to make kneading possible.

☐ Use flour with a high gluten content. Gluten, the protein in flour, absorbs water, and the higher the gluten content the more elastic the dough and the lighter the finished loaf. High gluten flour is usually labelled Strong Bread Flour.

☐ Add the yeast in the correct manner for the type of yeast used.

Fresh yeast is usually creamed with a little sugar or honey – about 1 teaspoon for 30–60 g/1–2 oz yeast – until the mixture is smooth, when about one third of the liquid is added. The yeast is then left for 15 minutes to grow before it is added to the other ingredients. Sometimes one third of the flour is added to make a yeast sponge.

Dried granular yeast is reconstituted with sugar and a quarter of the liquid. This mixture is left to froth, then the dough is made. It is important to mix the yeast granules thoroughly into the water to prevent lumps forming.

Easy blend or instant yeast is added to the dry ingredients – flour, sugar and salt – and then all the liquid is added at once. The dough must be well kneaded to distribute the yeast evenly.

☐ Knead the dough thoroughly. This part of bread making causes the most groans, but kneading dough can be very satisfying, once you have developed a rhythm.

Stretch the dough away from you using the heel of your hand, then gather it up into a ball and continue until the dough is even and elastic. Once you have made bread a few times you will recognize the feel of well kneaded dough. It is smooth and elastic. Quite simply, it feels good!

Children make very good bread, because they can be as rough as they like and still get good results. Most children love kneading the dough into fantastic shapes, as they get all the fun of modelling with an edible result.

☐ Most bread needs two periods of rising: the first and longest rising after the dough has been made, and the second rising after the dough has been shaped. You can shape the dough initially and allow it to rise only once, but the result will not be as fine as after a double rising.

As the yeast grows in the dough, bubbles of carbon dioxide are given off, causing it to expand. The warmer the temperature the faster the dough will rise, so for a quick rise

I place the dough, oiled and covered, on top of my boiler. For a slower rise I choose a warm, draughtfree spot, and for an overnight rise, to give fresh bread for breakfast, I put the dough in the bottom of the fridge.

Always cover the dough to prevent a dry crust forming.

□ Bread is always baked in a hot oven, usually at about 220°C/425°F/Gas 7. This kills the yeast and so stops the rising process. To test that the bread is cooked, turn the loaf over and tap the bottom. A hollow sound means the bread is ready. If you have removed the loaf from a tin to test it, return it to the oven shelf without its tin to crisp the crust.

□ Bread can be baked in a variety of tins and moulds. I use loaf tins of various sizes, baking trays, Continental baking moulds and even flowerpots, seasoned and kept for the purpose. The chosen tin should be half filled with the dough before the second rising to allow enough space for the dough to rise level with the top of the tin.

□ Once the bread is done, allow it to cool on a wire rack, then wrap and store in a bread tin, or freeze until needed.

Basic white bread dough

675 g/1½ lb strong flour
1 teaspoon salt
1 packet easy blend yeast
2 tablespoons vegetable oil
about 420 ml/¾ pint warm water

This dough is good for pizza bases, breakfast rolls, hand flattened breads to cook over barbecue coals, and staple white loaves.

You can make the dough richer by adding fat, milk and eggs in varying quantities but all these, and sugar too, will stop the yeast from working as efficiently, so it may be necessary to use extra yeast to combat this effect. For a rich sweet egg loaf I would double the yeast in this basic recipe.

Mix the salt, flour and yeast together, then add the oil and water. Stir well. The mixture should be soft but not sticky, and as flours vary it is difficult to be precise about the amount of water needed, but you should be able to work the dough quite easily with the addition of only a little extra flour.

Turn the dough on to a lightly floured board and knead for 5 minutes. An electric mixer with a dough hook or a food processor can be used. Cover the ball of dough and put to rise until doubled in size.

Knock back the dough and shape into whatever form you like. Allow the dough to rise for the second time, again covered with a damp cloth, then bake in a hot oven at 230°C/450°F/Gas 8. Baking time varies, depending on the size of the loaf. Rolls may take 10 minutes, and a large loaf about 30 minutes. Test the bread by tapping the base of the loaf: if done, the bread should give a hollow tone.

THREE-SEED WHOLEMEAL BREAD

500 g/1 lb 2 oz plain wholemeal flour
2 tablespoons sesame seeds
2 tablespoons sunflower seeds
1 teaspoon salt
1 sachet easy blend yeast
1 tablespoon oil
300 ml/½ pint warm water

to finish
a little milk
1 tablespoon poppy seeds

Homebaked wholemeal loaves are simple to make using easy blend yeast. I always put the dough to rise on top of the boiler with excellent results.

Mix the flour, seeds, salt and yeast together in a large bowl. Add the oil and water and stir well to form a dough. Turn this out on to a lightly floured board and knead for 5 minutes. The dough should be smooth and elastic.

Return the dough to the bowl and rub a little oil on the surface. Cover the bowl with a cloth and put in a warm place to double in size for 60–90 minutes.

Knock back the dough and divide into two halves. Knead each half lightly and shape into a round loaf. Put the two loaves on a greased baking sheet and cover with a cloth. Leave to rise again for about 30 minutes. Brush the loaves with milk and sprinkle on the poppy seeds.

Bake in a preheated oven at 230°C/450°F/Gas 8 for 30 minutes. The bread is done if it sounds hollow when the bottom is tapped. Allow to cool on a rack.

Foccacia

30 g/1 oz fresh yeast
½ teaspoon sugar
220 ml/8 fl oz hand-hot water
1 teaspoon sea salt
450 g/1 lb strong white bread flour
4 tablespoons fruity olive oil

to finish
olive oil, coarse salt

Mix the yeast with the sugar until it becomes creamy and then mix this into the water. Mix the salt with the flour, add the oil, yeast and water and mix together. Turn the dough out and knead on a floured board until smooth. Return to the bowl, cover with a cloth and put to rise in a warm place until the dough has doubled in size.

Heat the oven to 200°C/400°F/ Gas 6. Knock back the dough and knead lightly. Roll out the dough about 2 cm/¾ inch thick and place in a deep, well oiled tin about 30 × 20 cm/12 × 8 inches. Allow the dough to rise a second time and then with the handle of a wooden spoon make deep depressions into the dough about 5 cm/2 inches apart. Drizzle a further 2 tablespoons of oil over the surface and scatter on some coarse sea salt.

Bake the foccacia for 20–30 minutes until well risen and golden brown.

This is delicious served with any salad or antipasto.

Honey, date and oat bread

675 g/1½ lb strong wholemeal
  flour
1 tablespoon salt
225 g/8 oz medium oats
45 g/1½ oz fresh yeast
1 tablespoon clear honey
500 ml/scant pint warm water
225 g/8 oz chopped dates

This delicious bread needs cooking for a little longer than usual as the oats absorb water giving a moister loaf.

Mix the flour, salt, and oats together. Cream the yeast with the honey and mix in ¼ of the water plus 2 tablespoons of the flour mixture. Leave for 10 minutes until beginning to froth, and then add the remaining honey and water.

Mix this into the flour to give a softish dough. Turn out on to a floured surface and knead for about 5 minutes until smooth and elastic. Place in a bowl covered with a cloth and put in a warm place for about 2 hours to rise until double in size.

Knock back the dough, knead in the chopped dates and divide in half. Shape into loaves and place on a greased baking sheet. Cover and allow to rise again until doubled in size, about 30 minutes.

Bake the loaves in a hot oven at 230°C/450°F/Gas 8 for 30–40 minutes until the bread is well risen and lightly browned. Allow to cool on a rack. Freeze one loaf until needed.

POPPY SEED PICNIC BREAD RING

340 g/12 oz strong bread flour
1 sachet easy blend yeast
170 ml/6 fl oz warm milk and water
  mixed
1 tablespoon oil
1 teaspoon salt

to finish
beaten egg or milk
poppy seeds

Simple white bread rolls look more interesting when baked together in a cake tin to form one round loaf. At picnic time, each person pulls off as much as they need.

Mix together the flour, yeast, milk and water, oil and salt, and knead well. This can be done in a food processor. Cover the dough and put in a warm place to rise. When doubled in size knock it back and knead lightly for 2–3 minutes.

Divide the dough into 12 equal parts and knead each part into a round ball. Place the balls in a well greased 23 cm/9 inch cake tin. Put the dough to rise again, covered with a cloth. When the dough has risen to fill the tin, glaze the top with beaten egg or milk and sprinkle on the poppy seeds.

Bake in a preheated oven at 220°C/425°F/Gas 7 for 25–30 minutes until golden brown and a hollow sound is heard when the bottom is tapped.

Allow to cool. This bread freezes well.

CHOCOLATE BREAD

425 g/15 oz white bread flour
30 g/1 oz cocoa powder
1 teaspoon salt
1 packet easy blend yeast
115 g/4 oz chocolate chips
1 tablespoon muscovado sugar
1 tablespoon sunflower oil
300 ml/11 fl oz warm water

Admiring a wonderful display of breads in a well known Knightsbridge store, my eye was caught by a chocolate loaf, and I was reminded of a breakfast loaf I'd once eaten in Germany. This version can be eaten plain or with butter and may be lightly toasted, though I would suggest using a grill rather than the family toaster to avoid the chocolate chips melting on to the element.

Mix all the dry ingredients together, sieving the sugar if necessary to break up any lumps. Stir in the oil. Using as much water as necessary make a dough that is quite soft and a little sticky. On a floured board knead the dough for 5 minutes until smooth.

Place the ball of dough in a bowl covered with a cloth and put in a warm place to rise for about 1 hour until doubled in size. Knock back the dough and form it into a loaf. Place in a 900 g/2 lb loaf tin and allow to rise again for about 30 minutes.

Bake the bread in a preheated oven at 220°C/425°F/Gas 7 for 25–30 minutes, or until a hollow sound is heard when the base of the bread is tapped.

SUN-DRIED TOMATO AND HERB ROLLS

makes 8
225 g/8 oz plain flour
1 packet easy blend yeast
3 tablespoons milk
100 g/3½ oz butter, melted
½ teaspoon salt
2 eggs, beaten
1 teaspoon chopped herbs
(tarragon, oregano, rosemary)
beaten egg or milk for brushing
4 halves of oil-packed sun-dried
tomatoes, well drained

Make the dough by mixing all but the tomatoes in the bowl of a food processor for 1–2 minutes until a soft dough is formed. Turn this out on to a floured board and knead lightly for a few minutes. Place the ball of dough in a basin, cover with a damp cloth and leave to rise in a warm place for 1–2 hours.

When the dough has doubled in size, knock it back and knead for a further few minutes. Finely chop the tomatoes and knead these into the dough. You may need to add more flour as the tomatoes are oily.

Divide the dough into 8 pieces and shape these into balls. Place on a baking sheet and allow to rise, covered with a cloth. Preheat the oven to 250°C/475°F/Gas 9. When the rolls have doubled in size, brush with a little beaten egg and bake for 10–15 minutes until golden brown.

CHEESY POTATO BREAD ROLLS

makes 18–20
675 g/1½ lb strong white bread
flour
2 packets easy blend yeast
1 teaspoon salt
200 g/7 oz cold boiled potato
1½ tablespoons vegetable oil
200 ml/scant 8 fl oz each warm milk
and water, mixed

to finish
milk for brushing
140 g/5 oz Cheddar cheese, grated

The addition of cold mashed potato gives a soft texture to these rolls. Use a floury variety of potato and make sure there are no lumps!

Mix the flour, yeast, salt and potato together and add the oil, milk and water. Knead the dough on a lightly floured board for about 5 minutes, until smooth. Put the dough in a bowl, cover with a cloth and put it in a warm place to rise.

When the dough has doubled in size, after about 1 hour, knock it back and knead lightly. Divide the dough into 18–20 pieces and form into rolls. Place on a baking sheet, cover and leave to rise again, this time for about 30 minutes.

Heat the oven to 230°C/450°F/Gas 8. When the rolls have doubled in size, brush the tops with a little milk and sprinkle liberally with grated cheese.

Bake for 15–20 minutes, until well risen and golden brown. Allow to cool on a rack. These rolls freeze well.

ONION AND OLIVE LOAVES

makes 1 of each
675 g/1½ lb strong white bread
    flour
1 sachet easy blend yeast
1 teaspoon sea salt
2 tablespoons olive oil
420 ml/¾ pint/15 fl oz hand-hot
    water

to finish
1 large onion, chopped
1 tablespoon olive oil, plus extra
    for brushing
60 g/2 oz stoned black olives,
    coarsely chopped
coarse sea salt

Make the dough in the usual fashion: mix all the ingredients together and when combined, knead until the dough is soft and elastic. Cover with a clean cloth and put to rise until doubled in size.

Meanwhile, fry the onion in the oil until soft, then allow to cool.

Knock back the dough and divide into two parts. Knead the olives into one half and form into an oval loaf. Place on a baking sheet. Knead the remaining dough, roll into a rectangle about 25 × 20 cm/10 × 8 inches and spread on the cooled onion and oil. Roll into a loaf shape. Placing the seam under the loaf, put on to the baking sheet.

Allow both loaves to rise until double in size and then brush with olive oil and sprinkle with coarse sea salt.

Bake in a preheated oven at 230°C/450°F/Gas 8 for 20–35 minutes, or until a hollow sound is heard when the base of the loaf is tapped. Carefully brush the surface of the loaves with a little more oil and allow to cool on a rack.

CINNAMON WALNUT ROLLS

makes 10
340 g/12 oz plain flour
1 sachet easy blend yeast
60 g/2 oz sugar
60 g/2 oz softened butter
½ teaspoon salt
110 ml/4 fl oz milk and water
   mixed
1 egg, beaten

for the topping
60 g/2 oz butter
60 g/2 oz brown sugar
60 g/2 oz walnuts

for the filling
2 tablespoons butter
60 g/2 oz caster sugar
2 tablespoons ground cinnamon

These sweet breakfast rolls are quite simple to make, but as the dough is rich, you must allow plenty of time for the yeast to work. The rolls cook together to form a caramel topped loaf, from which you break the individual portions.

Mix all the dough ingredients together. I use an electric mixer or food processor. When the dough is combined knead it for 5 minutes until smooth and elastic. Lightly oil the surface and put in a covered bowl in a warm place to rise. This may take 2 hours.

When the dough has doubled in size, make the topping. Melt the butter in a saucepan and dissolve the brown sugar in it. Add the walnuts. Tip this into a shallow 23 cm/9 inch round cake tin, and spread evenly over the base.

Knock back the dough and knead lightly. Roll the dough into a rectangle about 38 × 23 cm/ 15 × 9 inches. Spread this with the butter for the filling. Mix the sugar with the cinnamon, and sprinkle evenly over the buttered dough.

Roll up the dough as you would a Swiss roll, starting with the long side. Slice the roll into 10 × 4 cm/ 1½ inch pieces and arrange these flat in the tin on the topping. Cover and allow to rise for a further hour.

Bake the rolls in a preheated oven at 190°C/375°F/Gas 5 for 30–35 minutes, until they are golden brown in colour. As soon as you take the tin from the oven, invert it on to a plate to allow the sugar topping to run down into the rolls. After 5 minutes remove the tin and allow the rolls to cool. They can be warmed through before serving.

REFRIGERATOR ROLLS

makes 20–25 rolls
**675 g/1½ lb strong white bread
   flour**
1½ teaspoons salt
2 packets easy blend yeast
2 size 3 eggs, beaten
110 ml/4 fl oz warm water
220 ml/8 fl oz warm milk
60 g/2 oz butter, melted

to finish
poppy or sesame seeds, optional

*Though few things taste as good as
freshly baked bread for breakfast,
I for one have no desire to rise at
6 a.m. and prepare the dough. In
this recipe, the dough is prepared
in advance, then stored in the
fridge. Pinch off a small amount
each morning as required. It keeps
for 4–5 days, provided that the
demand for these delicious rolls
doesn't mean you use it all up
much sooner.*

Combine the flour, salt and yeast
in a large bowl. Mix together the
eggs, water, milk and butter, and
add to the flour. Mix well with a
wooden spoon, your hand or the
dough hook of an electric mixer.
Turn the dough out on to a lightly
floured board and knead well. The
dough will be sticky and you may
have to add a little extra flour, but
add only sufficient to enable you to
knead the bread. Oil the surface of
the dough, place in a large, clean
bowl and store in the bottom of
the fridge covered with a damp
cloth.

When you are ready to bake the
bread, break off a piece of the
dough, punch the rest down and
return it to the fridge. Knead the
piece of dough and divide into
rolls. Put on a baking sheet and
leave in a warm place to rise. This
may take up to 1 hour depending
on the size of the rolls and the
temperature of the dough.

Heat the oven to 230°C/450°F/
Gas 8. Brush the rolls with egg or
milk glaze, slash the tops with a
sharp knife and sprinkle with
poppy seeds or sesame seeds if
liked. Bake for 15–20 minutes,
until well risen, lightly browned
and a hollow sound is heard when
the bottom of a roll is tapped.

Walnut bread

450 g/1 lb wholemeal flour
225 g/8 oz strong white flour
2 packets easy blend yeast
1 teaspoon salt
115 g/4 oz coarsely chopped
  walnuts
1½ tablespoons oil
420 ml/¾ pint hot water

*This delicious bread is wonderful
with cheese or spread with butter
and honey at teatime.*

Mix the dry ingredients together
well. Add the oil and water and
mix to a dough. You may need a
little extra water as the dough
should be soft to handle.

Turn out on to a floured board
and knead for 5–10 minutes until
the dough becomes elastic. Place in
a covered bowl and put to rise in a
warm place.

When the dough has doubled in
size, after about 1 hour, knock it
back and divide into two pieces.
Knead these lightly and form
circular loaves. Place on a greased
baking sheet and put to rise again
for 30–40 minutes.

When doubled in size, bake in a
preheated oven at 230°C/450°F/
Gas 8 for 25–30 minutes. The
bread is cooked if it sounds hollow
when the base of the loaf is
tapped.

Allow to cool on a rack. As
bread freezes well you can wrap
and store the spare loaf until
needed.

Brioche buns

makes 10
225 g/8 oz plain flour
1 sachet easy blend yeast
3 tablespoons milk
100 g/3½ oz butter, melted
1 teaspoon caster sugar
½ teaspoon salt
2 size 2 eggs, beaten
beaten egg to glaze

*Freshly baked brioche is a real
breakfast treat. To save rising at
dawn to prepare the dough, mix
the night before and store in the
bottom of the fridge. Be sure to
allow the dough to warm to room
temperature and finish rising
before baking.*

Place all the ingredients in a bowl
or food processor, and mix until
smooth. If mixing by hand turn
out on to a lightly floured board
and knead for 3–4 minutes. The
dough will be sticky. Place in a
lightly oiled polythene bag and
leave to rise either in a warm place
for 1–2 hours or overnight in the
fridge.

Knock back the dough and
divide into 10 pieces. Pinch a small
piece of dough from each one. Roll
the large pieces of dough into
balls, topping each one with a
small ball.

Place in deep bun tins and brush
well with beaten egg to glaze.
Allow to rise for 30 minutes, and
when double in size, bake in a
preheated oven at 220°C/425°F/
Gas 7 for 10–15 minutes.

SALMON AND PESTO BRIOCHE BUNS

makes 12
225 g/8 oz plain flour
1 packet easy blend yeast
3 tablespoons milk
100 g/3½ oz butter, melted
1 teaspoon sugar
½ teaspoon salt
2 eggs, beaten

for the filling
100 g/3½ oz pesto (basil sauce,
  either bought or homemade)
285 g/10 oz cold cooked salmon
beaten egg to glaze

Although these are best baked the day they are to be eaten, much of the preparation can be done in advance.

Put all the ingredients for the dough into the bowl of a food processor and mix well for 2–3 minutes. Turn the rather sticky dough out on to a floured board and knead it lightly with the flat of your hand, then pat and turn it into a ball.

Put it in a greased polythene bag and leave to rise either in a warm place for 2 hours or overnight in the fridge. Knock back the dough and divide it into 12 balls. Knead each one lightly, then roll them out into circles about 10 cm/4 inches in diameter.

Place a small spoonful of pesto in the centre of each circle, then put on a piece of the cold salmon. Moisten the edges of the dough, then gather the dough round the filling to form a ball. Place seam side down on a baking sheet and leave to rise for about 15 minutes while the oven is heating to 230°C/450°F/Gas 8.

Glaze with beaten egg and bake for about 15 minutes until golden brown. Allow to cool.

Glazed doughnuts

makes 15–20
450 g/1 lb plain flour
1 sachet easy blend yeast
½ teaspoon salt
1 tablespoon sugar
30 g/1 oz butter, melted
200 ml/7 fl oz warm milk and water
  mixed

to finish
170 g/6 oz icing sugar
water to mix
oil for frying

I have finally found a yeast dough that makes wonderfully light doughnuts.

Mix the dry ingredients together and add the melted butter along with the milk and water mixture. Stir until you have incorporated the liquid, then turn out on to a lightly floured board and knead the dough for about 5 minutes until smooth. Return the dough to the bowl, cover and put in a warm place until doubled in size.

Knock back the dough and roll out to about 2 cm/¾ inch thick. Cut 8 cm/3 inch circles and cut a hole in the centre of each. Re-roll the trimmings. Allow the doughnuts to rise for about 10 minutes. Mix together the sugar and water to make a thin icing and heat the cooking oil.

Deep fry the doughnuts in hot oil for 4–5 minutes each side, until well risen and golden. Remove and drain on kitchen paper.

Dip the warm doughnuts into the icing. Allow to cool on a rack.

Bara brith

450 g/1 lb strong white flour
1 packet easy blend yeast
85 g/3 oz soft brown sugar
1 teaspoon salt
1 teaspoon mixed spice
1 size 2 egg
85 g/3 oz melted butter
220 ml/8 fl oz warm milk
340 g/12 oz dried fruit

to finish
clear honey

The recipe for this Welsh teatime treat was given to me by Nellie Kirkby of Porthcawl.

Mix together the flour, yeast, sugar, salt and spice, beat the egg and combine with the butter and milk. Add this mixture to the dry ingredients and beat well. Turn the dough out on to a board and knead for 5–10 minutes. You may need to use about 30 g/1 oz extra flour, as the dough is quite sticky. Replace the dough in the bowl, cover and put to rise for 1½–2 hours until double in size.

Knock back the dough and knead in the fruit. Shape into an oblong and roll up, starting with the short side, to make a loaf. Place in a well greased 900 g/2 lb loaf tin, cover and put to rise until the dough peeps above the tin.

Bake in a preheated oven at 200°C/400°F/Gas 6 for 45–55 minutes. You may cover the top with paper or foil if it becomes too brown. When the bread is cooked, remove from the oven and brush the top with a little clear honey.

LARDY CAKE

170–340 g/6–12 oz lard
450 g/1 lb strong white flour
1 teaspoon salt
1 packet easy blend yeast
275 ml/½ pint milk
170 g/6 oz caster sugar
225 g/8 oz mixed dried fruit

This is an unashamedly indulgent lardy cake made with yeast dough filled with fruit. It was traditionally baked on the pig farms of Wiltshire where lard was more plentiful than butter.

I leave it up to you to choose how much lard you wish to use: from 170 g/6 oz for those who like a lighter cake, to a full 340 g/12 oz for a cake for true addicts that should carry a government health warning.

Rub 30 g/1 oz lard into the flour and salt and then add the yeast and milk and knead for about 5 minutes, until you have a smooth dough. This can be done in a food processor. Cover and put in a warm place to rise for about 2 hours, until doubled in size.

Knock back the dough, and on a floured board roll it into a rectangle about 36 × 20 cm/ 14 × 8 inches. Spread two thirds of the dough nearest to you with the remaining lard and sprinkle with the sugar and fruit. Then, as if making puff pastry, turn the top third down and the bottom third up, press to seal the edges, give the dough a quarter turn and roll to a rectangle. Repeat the folding and rolling twice more, then roll the dough to fit a deep 30 × 20 cm/ 12 × 8 inch baking tin. Put the dough, in the tin, in a warm place to rise until doubled in size. Bake in a preheated oven at 220°C/ 425°F/Gas 7 for about 45 minutes, until well risen and golden brown.

When you take the cake from the oven it will be swimming in fat. Carefully turn the cake over in the tin, sprinkle with a little caster sugar and allow it to cool. The fat will be absorbed by the dough.

Remove from the tin when cold and cut into thin slices. This lardy cake freezes well.

CHAPTER
4

*Pastry making
&
pies*

THE CRUST ON the earliest pies was nothing more than a protection for the filling against the fierce heat of the oven, and meant to be discarded when the pie was eaten. Cinder-specked pastry cases, though inedible, made food easily portable for travelling and on such outings as hunts, and pies continue to be popular for taking to work and on picnics.

Cornish pasties were eaten by the tin miners, who would always save a corner of the pastry and leave it for the spirit of the mine, to ward off bad luck. In Argentina, gauchos eat empanadas, their own variation on the pasty, while they are out herding cattle. In India samosas are sold on every street corner, and these savoury pastry envelopes are now becoming increasingly popular in England.

Shortcrust, filo, choux, and puff pastries all appear in this chapter used in many different ways. I always make my own shortcrust pastry, having devised a foolproof recipe, and sometimes I make the richer French version, pâte brisée, or its sweet cousin, pâte sucrée. Wherever I have specified shortcrust in the recipes that follow, you can use whichever one of these you please. I only occasionally make puff pastry, and usually use ready made puff, which is available at most supermarkets. However, I do give a recipe here, in case you have the time to make it at home.

Choux, though not strictly pastry as we know it, is always freshly made and can be used in a variety of savoury as well as sweet dishes. Making filo or strudel pastry is a-once-in-a-lifetime experience. It may be interesting to try, but I always buy filo fresh or frozen, and recommend that you do the same.

When it comes to making pastry, lightness is very important if you don't wish the pie crust to suffer the same fate as its ancestors. Remember not to over-handle the dough. Pastry making is the opposite of bread making: the idea is not to work the flour and stretch the gluten, but to achieve a crisp light finish.

SHORTCRUST PASTRY

225 g/8 oz butter
30 g/1 oz lard
450 g/1 lb plain flour
a pinch of salt
1 egg, beaten
cold water

I always make my pastry with butter: I don't eat pies too often and I love the flavour of rich buttery pastry when I do. For preference I use concentrated cooking butter, which is usually less costly than other butters and keeps well in the freezer. I always make pastry in batches to use 450 g/1 lb flour, and freeze any I don't need at once. Use a food processor for perfect results.

For a sweet flan pastry I add 1 tablespoon each of cornflour and icing sugar to the original recipe.

Cut the cold fats into small cubes and place with the flour and salt in the food processor bowl. Use a metal blade to cut the fat into the flour until the mixture resembles breadcrumbs. I then tip the mixture into a large mixing bowl. You can add the egg and water in the processor, but adding it by hand gives a more predictable result.

Beat the egg with about 4 tablespoons water, sprinkle it over the flour mixture and cut it in with a knife. If the mixture doesn't seem to want to hold together, add a little more water. Once it starts to stick, use your hands to quickly and lightly knead it into a ball. Wrap in polythene and leave to rest in a cool place for 30 minutes.

PÂTE BRISÉE

170 g/6 oz plain flour
½ teaspoon salt
2 egg yolks
125 g/4½ oz butter
cold water if necessary

I make this pâte brisée in a bowl, though it is traditionally made on a marble slab.

French pastry is usually richer than our shortcrust, as egg yolk is often used instead of water to bind the mixture. Pâte brisée is a savoury pastry, and pâte sucrée (below) a very rich sweet one. In both cases, the dough is kneaded with the heel of the hand until it is smooth and pliable.

In a large mixing bowl, sift the flour with the salt. Make a well in the centre and put in the egg yolks. Work the butter on a board with a palette knife until malleable, then add to the yolks.

Mix the butter, flour and eggs together with one hand, until they form large lumps. This is a bit messy to begin with. Once the pastry starts to stick together, form it into a ball and turn out on to a lightly floured board. If the dough will not stick together easily, moisten with a little water.

Knead the dough as you would for bread for 1–2 minutes until the pastry is a good even colour and texture. Place in a polythene bag and refrigerate for 30 minutes before using.

Pâte sucrée

200 g/7 oz plain flour
¼ teaspoon salt
115 g/4 oz caster sugar
115 g/4 oz butter
3–4 egg yolks

This pastry is used for making fruit tarts and most sweet patisserie.

Make as for pâte brisée, above, using the extra egg yolk if necessary to bind the dough.

Puff pastry

200 g/7 oz butter
285 g/10 oz plain flour, sifted
a pinch of salt
about 275 ml/½ pint cold water

Puff or flaky pastry is used in many ways, one of which is to make the traditional French pastry mille feuilles, literally, one thousand leaves. I calculate that this method gives you 729 leaves.

Work the butter until it is soft, then divide into four. Take one quarter of the butter and rub it into the flour and salt. Add just enough water to make a soft dough. The dough should not be sticky.

Knead lightly, then form the dough into a ball. Roll out an oblong about 30 × 10 cm/ 12 × 4 inches, and place short side towards you on the board.

Take a further quarter of the butter and place dabs of it, evenly spaced, over the top two thirds of the dough.

Fold the bottom third of pastry up, and then the top third down, enclosing the butter. Press with a rolling pin to seal the edges and then give the dough a quarter turn. Re-roll to give an oblong 30 × 10 cm/12 × 4 inches and repeat the above steps until all the fat is used.

Re-roll the dough, folding and turning as above twice more, then place in the fridge for 30 minutes before using.

Tarte aux noix

125 g/4½ oz butter
255 g/9 oz plain flour, sifted
a pinch of salt
30 g/1 oz icing sugar
1 egg

for the filling
115 g/4 oz butter
115 g/4 oz caster sugar
2 size 2 eggs, beaten
50 g/scant 2 oz flour
115 g/4 oz chopped walnuts

to finish
115 g/4 oz plain chocolate
2 tablespoons double cream

Make a pâte sucrée by rubbing the butter into the flour, salt and sugar and forming a dough with the egg. Knead lightly until smooth and then chill for 1 hour.

Roll out the pastry and line a 20 cm/8 inch flan tin. For the filling, cream the butter with the sugar, add the egg a little at a time, and fold in the flour and nuts. Spoon the filling into the pie and bake in a preheated oven at 200°C/400°F/Gas 6 for 25 minutes, or until the pastry is golden and the filling cooked.

Remove from the oven and allow to cool. When the pie is cold, melt the chocolate with the cream and stir well. Spread evenly over the pie.

Molasses and coconut rum tart

225 g/8 oz shortcrust pastry (page 71)
275 ml/½ pint soured cream
4 size 2 eggs
225 g/8 oz molasses sugar (raw cane)
2 tablespoons rum
½ teaspoon vanilla essence
115 g/4 oz desiccated coconut

This tart has the wonderfully rich flavour of raw sugar.

Line a 23 cm/9 inch flan tin with the pastry.

Beat the filling ingredients together and pour into the pastry case. Bake for 35–40 minutes in a preheated oven at 200°C/400°F/Gas 6, until the pastry is brown and the filling set.

Serve warm or cold with cream.

PEACH, ALMOND AND CURD CHEESE TART

4–5 large ripe peaches
225 g/8 oz ready made puff pastry
85 g/3 oz caster sugar
115 g/4 oz curd cheese
2 size 2 eggs, separated
60 g/2 oz ground almonds
¼ teaspoon vanilla essence

This simple tart is made with juicy ripe peaches laid on a thin puff pastry base and covered with a frangipani of curd cheese and almonds.

If desired, peel the peaches by dipping into boiling water for 60 seconds and slipping off the skins.

Roll the pastry out very thinly and use to line a Swiss roll tin about 36 × 30 cm/14 × 12 inches. Slice the fruit thinly and arrange over the pastry.

Beat together the sugar, cheese, egg yolks, almonds and vanilla. Whisk the whites until stiff, then fold in the yolk mixture. Spread this in an even layer over the peach slices, sprinkle with a little extra sugar, then bake in a preheated oven at 200°C/400°F/Gas 6 for 35–45 minutes, until the topping is well browned and the pastry cooked.

Serve warm.

ORANGE AND ALMOND TART

225 g/8 oz shortcrust pastry (page 71)

for the filling
4 small oranges
3 eggs, beaten
170 g/6 oz caster sugar
125 g/4½ oz ground almonds

Serve this tart warm with ice cream. Lemon ice cream (page 120) is particularly good.

Line a 20 cm/8 inch flan tin with the pastry.

Grate the rind from 2 oranges, then squeeze the juice from 3. Mix the rind and juice with the remaining ingredients for the filling and pour into the pie shell. Finely slice the remaining orange and arrange on top of the orange mixture. Bake in the centre of a preheated oven at 180°C/360°F/Gas 4 for 40 minutes, or until the crust is brown and the filling set.

Strawberry and Almond Tart

675 g/1½ lb ripe strawberries
225 g/8 oz pâte sucrée (page 72)

for the filling
100 g/3½ oz blanched or ground almonds
100 g/3½ oz butter
100 g/3½ oz caster sugar
1 egg plus 1 yolk
1 tablespoon plain flour
1 tablespoon almond liqueur, optional

to finish
4 tablespoons apple or redcurrant jelly

This delicious tart makes the most of your strawberries, and as the frangipani base is rich it doesn't need cream.

The tart may be baked ahead but the strawberries and glaze should not be added until just before eating.

Line a 23 cm/9 inch tart tin with the pastry.

To make the filling, place the almonds in a food processor and process until finely ground. Add the remaining ingredients, and process well.

If you are making this tart without a processor use ground almonds. Cream the fat with the sugar, add the eggs, then combine with the flour, almonds and liqueur.

Pour the frangipani into the pastry case and bake in a pre-heated oven at 180°C/360°F/Gas 4 for 30–35 minutes until the top is golden and the pastry cooked. Allow to cool.

Carefully place the prepared strawberries in circles on the tart, continuing until the surface is covered. Melt the jelly with 1 teaspoon water and brush over the tart.

TARTE TATIN

60 g/2 oz butter
60 g/2 oz caster sugar
**3–4 dessert apples, peeled and
   sliced**
225 g/8 oz ready made puff pastry

*I make no claims that this is a
genuine Tarte Tatin, but it is
delicious and very simple to
assemble. I use an enamelled cast
iron gratin dish to make this tart.
It works wonderfully well, but
needs a little more care when you
come to turn out the finished dish.*

Over a medium flame melt the
butter in a 20 cm/8 inch cast iron
dish. Add the sugar and stirring
constantly, cook until you have a
light golden caramel. This will take
about 5 minutes. Remove from the
heat at once and add the apple
slices.

   Roll the pastry out to fit the dish
and arrange on top of the apple
slices.

   Bake in a preheated oven at
220°C/425°F/Gas 7 for 20–25
minutes, until the pastry is well
risen and golden. Allow to cool for
1–2 minutes, then carefully turn
out on to a serving dish. Spoon
over any remaining caramel.

   Serve warm with thick cream.

APPLE MERINGUE PIE

**225 g/8 oz shortcrust pastry (page
   71)**
2 large Bramley apples
2 eggs, separated
**1 tablespoon brandy, 2
   tablespoons marmalade or 1
   teaspoon ground cinnamon**
85 g/3 oz caster sugar

Line a 20 cm/8 inch flan dish with
the pastry, cover with a sheet of
greaseproof and put in some
baking beans. Bake the pastry shell
for 15 minutes in a preheated oven
at 180°C/360°F/Gas 4. Remove the
beans.

   Peel, core and slice the apples
and cook them in a very little
water until you have a thick purée.
Allow this to cool slightly, then
beat in the egg yolks, and then
either the brandy, marmalade or
cinnamon. Pour into the pie shell.

   Whisk the egg whites until stiff
and then whisk in the caster sugar.
Pile this on to the apple purée and
return to the oven at 180°C/360°F/
Gas 4 for 20 minutes, until the
meringue is lightly browned.

   Allow to cool a little before
serving.

Banana cream pie

225 g/8 oz shortcrust pastry (page 71)
2 egg yolks
4–5 tablespoons caster sugar
2 tablespoons cornflour
420 ml/¾ pint creamy milk
1 teaspoon vanilla essence
275 ml/½ pint whipping cream
4–5 ripe bananas
grated chocolate or almonds to decorate

This fragile pie is best assembled not more than one hour before serving.

Line a 23 cm/9 inch flan tin with the pastry, cover with a sheet of greaseproof and put in some baking beans. Bake in a preheated oven at 180°C/360°F/Gas 4 for 15 minutes. Remove the beans. Continue to bake for 20 minutes or until the base is golden brown. Allow to cool.

Mix together the egg yolks, sugar and cornflour, adding a little milk if needed to give a smooth cream. Scald the remaining milk, and when it reaches boiling point, pour a few tablespoons into the egg mixture and mix in. Add the remaining hot milk, stir well and return the custard to the pan. Over a low to moderate flame, cook the custard, stirring constantly, until it thickens and bubbles appear on the surface. Allow the custard to simmer for about 60 seconds to cook the cornflour.

Remove from the heat, strain into a clean bowl, mix in the vanilla and leave to cool, stirring occasionally to prevent a skin from forming.

When the custard has cooled, whip the cream to soft peaks and fold in to the custard. Peel and slice the bananas. Place half the cream in the pie shell and cover with banana, then top with the remaining cream. Sprinkle on the chocolate or almonds.

BAKEWELL PUDDING

225 g/8 oz shortcrust pastry
5 tablespoons raspberry jam
5 tablespoons lemon curd
140 g/5 oz caster sugar
140 g/5 oz softened butter
2 large eggs, beaten
1 teaspoon almond essence
85 g/3 oz ground almonds
60 g/2 oz self-raising flour
30 g/1 oz pinenuts, optional

This Bakewell pudding has both raspberry jam and lemon curd to give a sweeter tangy flavour. Southerners tend to call it 'Bakewell tart', much to the annoyance of the inhabitants of Bakewell, who know best, after all.

Line a 23 cm/9 inch flan tin with the pastry. Spread raspberry jam on the pastry and cover with a layer of lemon curd. In a mixing bowl cream the sugar with the butter, then gradually beat in the eggs. Add the almond essence and fold in the ground almonds and flour. Spread the mixture over the jam layers and sprinkle with pinenuts, if you like.

Bake in a preheated oven at 190°C/375°F/Gas 5 for 45–55 minutes, or until the pastry is cooked and the filling well risen and golden brown. Remove from the oven and allow to cool, then remove from the tin.

CINNAMON, APRICOT AND SOURED CREAM FLAN

225 g/8 oz shortcrust pastry (page 71)
400 g/14 oz tin apricots, drained
270 ml/½ pint soured cream
3 size 2 eggs, beaten
60 g/2 oz soft brown sugar
1 teaspoon cinnamon

This flan makes good use of store cupboard ingredients.

Line a deep 20 cm/8 inch flan tin with the pastry and arrange the apricot halves over the base. Beat together the remaining ingredients and pour carefully over the fruit.

Bake in a preheated oven at 180°C/360°F/Gas 4 for 35–40 minutes. Serve warm.

APPLE CRUNCH TART

225 g/8 oz shortcrust pastry (page 71)
3–4 large cooking apples
grated rind and juice of ½ lemon
sugar to taste

for the topping
115 g/4 oz plain flour
85 g/3 oz caster sugar
85 g/3 oz butter

This tart is simply flavoured with apple and lemon.

Line a deep 20 cm/8 inch flan dish with the pastry and trim the edges. Peel the apples and slice on to the pastry. Sprinkle the fruit with the lemon rind, juice and sugar to taste.

Rub the topping ingredients together until the mixture resembles fine crumbs, then sprinkle evenly over the apples.

Bake in a preheated oven at 200°C/400°F/Gas 6 for 40–50 minutes, or until the pastry is cooked and the topping a light golden brown. Serve with cream or ice cream.

AMERICAN APPLE PIE

450 g/1 lb shortcrust pastry (page 71)
900 g/2 lb cooking apples
rind and juice of 1 lemon
115–170 g/4–6 oz caster sugar
¼ teaspoon salt
2 teaspoons cinnamon
½ teaspoon grated nutmeg
60 g/2 oz butter
milk and sugar to glaze

I was amazed when I first heard the expression, widely used in the USA, 'as American as apple pie', as I had foolishly imagined apple pie to be a British dish. This recipe, for a deep dish country style pie as favoured by the Pennsylvania Dutch, is flavoured with lemon, cinnamon and nutmeg. Serve it 'à la mode' with vanilla ice cream.

Line a deep ovenproof dish with half the pastry, and roll out the remainder to form a lid.

Peel and slice the apples into a large bowl. Mix in the lemon rind, juice, sugar, salt and spices, and toss well. Tip into the pie case and dot with butter.

Dampen the edges of the pastry and cover with the lid. Press to seal. Cut two vents in the top crust and brush with milk. Sprinkle generously with sugar, and bake the pie in a preheated oven at 180°C/360°F/Gas 4 for 45–60 minutes, until the pastry is golden.

Serve warm with cream or ice cream.

FRESH FIG TARTS

makes 6
340 g/12 oz ready made puff pastry
140 ml/¼ pint double cream
6 large or 9–10 medium sized fresh figs
caster sugar

These fig tarts are quite beautiful to look at. They are simple to make and taste best fresh from the oven.

Roll out the pastry, cut 6 × 10 cm/ 4 inch circles, and place on a baking sheet. Brush each circle with a spoonful of double cream. Carefully peel the dark skin from the figs and slice into 5 mm/¼ inch rings. Share the fruit between the pastry circles, leaving a 1 cm/½ inch rim round the edge. At this stage you can cover the tray loosely with cling film and leave in the fridge for 2–3 hours.

Preheat the oven to 220°C/ 425°F/Gas 7, sprinkle the tarts with sugar and bake for 10–15 minutes, or until the pastry is puffy and golden brown. Serve at once with the remaining cream.

SOURED CREAM AND PECAN PIE

285 g/10 oz shortcrust pastry (page 71)
60 g/2 oz butter
170 g/6 oz soft brown sugar
140 ml/¼ pint soured cream
3 size 3 eggs, beaten
¼ teaspoon salt
1 teaspoon vanilla
140 g/5 oz pecans (or walnuts)

On Thanksgiving Day Americans worldwide gather to celebrate together, and to eat, amongst other things, pecan pie. I am giving three different recipes for you to try.

Line a 23 cm/9 inch dish with the pastry. Beat the butter and sugar together, and then beat in the cream, eggs, salt and vanilla. This can be done in a food processor. Add the nuts and chop roughly, or chop the nuts and stir in. Reserve a few whole nuts to decorate, if liked.

Pour the mixture into the pie shell, and bake in a preheated oven at 180°C/360°F/Gas 4 for 40–45 minutes, until the pastry is cooked and the filling set.

Serve warm or cold with cream.

MAPLE PECAN PIE

285 g/10 oz shortcrust pastry (page 71)
3 large eggs
220 ml/8 fl oz maple syrup
60 g/2 oz caster sugar
½ teaspoon salt
1 tablespoon butter
170 g/6 oz roughly chopped pecans (if not available use walnuts)
1 tablespoon flour

Line a 23 cm/9 inch flan tin with the pastry.

Beat the eggs with the maple syrup and sugar. Add the remaining ingredients and stir well. Pour into the pie shell and bake in a preheated oven at 200°C/400°F/Gas 6 for 15 minutes, and then at 190°C/375°F/Gas 5 for a further 30 minutes. The filling will be set, though less firm in the centre. Serve warm with thick cream.

CHOCOLATE PECAN PIE

340 g/12 oz shortcrust pastry
140 g/5 oz plain chocolate
225 g/8 oz pecans (or walnuts)
4 size 3 eggs, beaten
170 g/6 oz caster sugar
220 ml/8 fl oz corn syrup (not golden syrup)
60 g/2 oz butter, melted

Line a deep 23 cm/9 inch loose bottomed flan dish with the pastry, cover with a sheet of greaseproof and put in some baking beans. Bake the pastry shell for 15 minutes at 180°C/360°F/Gas 4. Remove the beans.

Chop the chocolate and put it, with the nuts, into the pie. Beat together the remaining ingredients and pour over. Return the pie to the oven at the same setting for a further 50–60 minutes or until the top is a deep gold and the filling almost set.

Allow to cool, remove from the tin and serve cold.

PUMPKIN CHIFFON PIE

225 g/8 oz shortcrust pastry (page 71)
140 ml/¼ pint milk
1 envelope gelatine
2 eggs, separated
115 g/4 oz light brown sugar
½ teaspoon ground cinnamon
½ teaspoon freshly grated nutmeg
550 ml/1 pint pumpkin purée (see below)
60 g/2 oz caster sugar

Lighter than a custard style pumpkin pie, this chiffon pie is wonderfully spicy. Make the pumpkin purée by steaming 575 g/1¼ lb pumpkin, or by cooking in a microwave with 2 tablespoons water.

Line a 23 cm/9 inch pie dish with the pastry, cover with a sheet of greaseproof and put in some baking beans. Bake for 15 minutes, or until completely cooked, in a preheated oven at 180°C/360°F/Gas 4. Remove the beans, and continue cooking until the base is golden. Allow to cool.

Warm the milk and dissolve the gelatine in it. Beat the egg yolks, the brown sugar and the spices into the pumpkin mixture and add the milk. Mix well and leave until the mixture begins to set.

Beat the egg whites with the caster sugar until stiff, and fold this into the setting pumpkin mixture. Pour into the pie shell and chill for at least 2 hours.

CHOCOLATE-FILLED PEARS
in puff pastry

4 large ripe dessert pears
115 g/4 oz plain chocolate
450 g/1 lb puff pastry
beaten egg
sugar

These chocolate-filled pears are easy to make using ready made puff pastry.

Peel each pear, leaving the stalk, then carefully remove the core from below. Divide the chocolate between the pears, pushing it up inside them.

Divide the pastry into four and roll each piece into a square about 18 cm/7 inches across. Place a pear in the centre of each square and gather up the pastry to enclose the fruit, pressing to seal the edges. Neaten the pastry around the stalk if necessary.

Stand the pears on a greased baking sheet, brush with egg and bake in a preheated oven at 200°C/400°F/Gas 6 for 25 minutes, or until lightly browned. Remove from the oven, brush again with the egg and sprinkle with sugar. Return to the oven and cook until golden brown.

Serve warm with cream.

MINCEMEAT AND ALMOND JALOUSIE

2 × 225 g/8 oz pieces frozen puff pastry, thawed
60 g/2 oz slivered almonds
1 tablespoon brandy
1½ jars mincemeat (about 675 g/ 1½ lb)
beaten egg and sugar to glaze

The pastry top of this mincemeat pie is cut and arranged to resemble a Venetian blind, in French, jalousie. This dish freezes well.

Roll each piece of pastry into an oblong about 36 × 18 cm/ 14 × 7 inches. Lay one piece on a baking tray. Fold the other piece in half to make a long narrow strip. Carefully cut lines about 2 cm/¾ inch apart along the length of the strip and through both thicknesses of pastry, starting with a cut through the folded edge, but leaving 1 cm/½ inch border at the open edge. Carefully unfold the pastry and you should, with luck, have an oblong that resembles a Venetian blind hanging in a 1 cm/ ½ inch frame of uncut pastry.

Mix the nuts and brandy into the mincemeat and spread this evenly on the uncut sheet, leaving 1 cm/½ inch border clear. Dampen this border and carefully lay on the cut pastry top. Seal the edges and brush the jalousie with beaten egg. Sprinkle with sugar and bake in a preheated oven at 200°C/400°F/ Gas 6 for 30–40 minutes, until the pastry is puffy and golden brown.

Allow to cool. Serve with cream.

CUSTARD TART

225 g/8 oz shortcrust pastry (page 71)
3 size 3 eggs
275 ml/½ pint creamy milk
2 tablespoons caster sugar
½ teaspoon vanilla essence
freshly grated nutmeg

This is one of my favourite puddings. I always bake the pastry case blind before adding the egg and milk mixture so the finished tart has a crisp base.

Roll out the pastry about 5 mm/ ¼ inch thick and line a loose bottomed 20 cm/8 inch flan dish. Cover the base with greaseproof paper and baking beans then bake in a preheated oven at 190°C/ 375°F/Gas 5 for 15 minutes, or until the pastry is set but not brown. Remove the beans and paper.

Beat together the filling ingredients and strain into the pie shell. Grate lots of nutmeg over the surface and return to the oven. Cook for a further 25–35 minutes until the custard is set. Allow to cool before serving.

BAKLAVA

170 g/6 oz honey
170 ml/⅓ pint water
juice of ½ lemon
60 g/2 oz butter
6 large sheets filo pastry
200 g/7 oz finely chopped nuts

This baklava is not quite authentic as I prefer to use less sugar and butter than the original Greek recipe. Use a scented honey or add 1 teaspoon rosewater to the cooked syrup.

Dissolve the honey in the water and boil the syrup for 5 minutes. Add the lemon juice and allow to cool.

Melt the butter and brush the bottom of your chosen pan: I use a shallow 30 × 15 cm/12 × 6 inch baking tin. Lay one sheet of filo on this and brush with butter. Cover with two more sheets, buttering well each time. Sprinkle the chopped nuts over the pastry and cover with two more sheets of well buttered filo.

Before you put on the last layer, turn in all the ragged edges and butter them down. Fold the last sheet of filo to size and place on top, brushing with the remaining butter. Cut the baklava into diamond shapes with a sharp knife.

Bake in a preheated oven at 180°C/360°F/Gas 4 for 20 minutes, then turn down the heat to 160°C/325°F/Gas 3 and cook for a further 20–30 minutes, until the baklava is golden brown.

Remove from the oven and pour over the syrup as evenly as possible. Allow to cool, then remove from the tin.

Basic choux paste

70 g/2½ oz plain flour
a pinch of salt
140 ml/¼ pint water
60 g/2 oz butter
2 size 3 eggs, beaten

More of a batter than a traditional pastry, choux needs no rubbing in, no resting in a cool place and no rolling out. The paste can be flavoured in a variety of ways and baked or deep-fried. If baked, it is usually put into a very hot oven for 10 minutes to give maximum rise, then the temperature is lowered for the remainder of the cooking time.

Sift the flour and the salt together and set aside.

In a heavy bottomed saucepan heat the water and butter until the butter has melted. Bring the liquid to a full rolling boil and then, all at once, tip in the flour. Remove the pan from the heat and beat the mixture well with a wooden spoon until you have a smooth ball and the sides of the saucepan are clean. If the dough is too wet, heat gently for a few moments, beating all the time. Allow the dough to cool for about 5 minutes.

Again with a wooden spoon, beat the eggs into the warm dough a little at a time, until the mixture is glossy but still stiff enough to hold its shape. If you are using eggs larger than size 3, you may not need to add all the beaten egg.

The choux paste is now ready to use. Keep the pan covered with a damp cloth until needed.

Profiteroles

basic choux paste (see left)
275 ml/½ pint double cream
200 g/7 oz tin sweetened chestnut
  purée
2 tablespoons brandy
85 g/3 oz plain chocolate
1 tablespoon butter
3–4 tablespoons boiling water

If you are unable to find sweetened purée use unsweetened purée sold for chestnut stuffing and beat in vanilla and icing sugar to taste.

Grease a baking sheet and drop spoonfuls of the choux paste on to it, well spaced. Bake in the centre of a preheated oven at 200°C/400°F/Gas 6 for 10 minutes, and then at 180°C/360°F/Gas 4 for a further 15–20 minutes, until puffed and golden brown. Remove from the oven and allow to cool on a rack.

Beat the cream until it holds soft peaks and then whip in the chestnut purée and brandy. Taste to check the sweetness. Fill a piping bag fitted with a plain nozzle with the mixture. Make small holes in the bottom of the choux puffs, and pipe each one full of cream.

Melt the chocolate with the butter in a bowl over simmering water. Mix well, then beat in the hot water 1 tablespoon at a time, until you have a smooth thick glossy sauce. Pour this over the filled profiteroles.

GOOSEBERRIES AND CREAM LATTICE TART

225 g/8 oz plain flour
1 tablespoon cornflour
1 tablespoon icing sugar
115 g/4 oz butter
1 egg beaten with 2 tablespoons
    iced water

for the filling
450 g/1 lb gooseberries
1 tablespoon flour
85 g/3 oz caster sugar, plus extra
    for sprinkling
140 ml/¼ pint single cream

Use thin-skinned gooseberries for this luscious and creamy tart. I also enjoy it filled with Champagne rhubarb when in season.

Make the pastry in the usual way, sieving the flour with the cornflour and icing sugar, and rubbing in the butter. Form into a dough with the egg and water mixture, reserving about 1 tablespoonful to glaze the tart. Line a deep 20 cm/8 inch tart dish with the pastry and re-roll the trimmings. Cut these into long strips.

Top, tail and wash the gooseberries. Mix the flour with the sugar, toss the gooseberries in it, then tip into the tart shell. Make a lattice top for the tart with the reserved strips of pastry. Brush with reserved egg and sprinkle on a little caster sugar.

Bake in a preheated oven at 200°C/400°F/Gas 6 for 30 minutes. Remove from the oven and carefully pour the cream into the tart through the gaps in the top. Return to the oven and bake for a further 15–20 minutes, until the pastry is crisp and brown and the cream has set. Serve warm.

LEMON MERINGUE PIE

**225 g/8 oz shortcrust pastry
(page 71)
2 large lemons
115 g/4 oz caster sugar
415 ml/¾ pint water
3 tablespoons cornflour
3 egg yolks**

for the meringue
**3 egg whites
170 g/6 oz caster sugar**

Line a 23 cm/9 inch pie dish with the pastry, cover with a sheet of greaseproof and put in some baking beans. Bake for 15 minutes at 180°C/360°F/Gas 4. Remove the beans. Continue to cook until the base is golden.

Scrub the lemons under hot water to remove the wax, then grate the rind finely. Squeeze the juice from the lemons and heat it with all but 3 tablespoons of the water and the caster sugar in a nonstick saucepan. Mix the remaining water with the cornflour and beat the egg yolks in.

When the water and lemon juice boils, pour it on to the egg and cornflour mixture, stirring well. Return to the saucepan, add the lemon rind and simmer for 2–3 minutes, until thickened. Pour into the pie shell and allow to cool.

For the meringue, whip the egg whites until stiff, beat in the caster sugar and carefully spoon or pipe it over the lemon filling. Bake in a preheated oven at 150°C/300°F/ Gas 2 for 30 minutes.

Allow to cool, then serve.

APPLE BEIGNETS
with cinnamon sugar

**2 dessert apples, peeled, cored and
chopped
basic choux pastry (page 85)
oil for frying
1 teaspoon ground cinnamon
mixed with 2 tablespoons sugar**

Fold the apple into the choux and deep-fry teaspoonfuls in hot oil, turning often until puffy and golden brown.

Drain and serve hot sprinkled with cinnamon sugar.

RASPBERRY AND CREAM CHOUX CROWN

60 g/2 oz butter
140 ml/¼ pint water
70 g/2½ oz plain flour
a pinch of salt
2 size 2 eggs, beaten
30 g/1 oz slivered almonds
275 ml/½ pint double cream
450 g/1 lb raspberries
sugar to taste
icing sugar

Place the butter and water in a saucepan and when the butter has melted bring the mixture to a rolling boil. Remove from the stove, add the flour and salt at once and beat with a wooden spoon. Allow the mixture to cool for 5 minutes, then beat in the eggs a little at a time.

Spoon the mixture on to a greased baking sheet to form a ring about 18 cm/7 inches in diameter. Sprinkle over the almonds.

Bake the choux in a preheated oven at 200°C/400°F/Gas 6 for 25–30 minutes, until risen and golden brown. Remove from the oven and allow to cool. When cold, slice off the top and remove any uncooked dough.

Beat the cream until stiff and fill the ring with this. Arrange the raspberries on top. Sprinkle with sugar. Replace the top of the choux ring and sprinkle generously with icing sugar.

SHOO FLY PIE

serves 8–10
225 g/8 oz shortcrust pastry
  (page 71)

for the crumble
85 g/3 oz butter
200 g/7 oz plain flour
140 g/5 oz soft brown sugar
a pinch of salt

for the filling
110 ml/4 fl oz black treacle
170 ml/6 fl oz boiling water
½ teaspoon bicarbonate of soda

This intriguingly named pie comes from the Pensylvannia Dutch kitchens of North America. One story says that when these pies were put on the window sill to cool a child had to sit beside them to shoo away the flies attracted by the sweet filling.

Line a deep 23 cm/9 inch pie dish with the pastry.

Rub the butter into the flour, sugar and salt to make the crumble. Put one third of the crumbs into the pie crust. Mix the treacle with the water and soda and pour over the crumbs. Sprinkle the remaining crumbs evenly over the top.

Bake in a preheated oven at 180°C/360°F/Gas 4 for 40–50 minutes, until the pastry is cooked and the crumb topping is well browned. Allow to cool and serve with ice cream or cream.

CHAPTER
5

Festive baking

One of the joys of Christmas is the wonderful smell that fills the house once the baking starts. I always make far too many cakes, pies and biscuits for us to eat and generosity being the spirit of the season, I give them to friends and neighbours.

Lent and Eastertide also have their traditions, from Shrove Tuesday pancakes to Shrewsbury biscuits, and marzipan-encrusted simnel cake.

Rich fruit Christmas cake

115 g/4 oz glacé cherries, washed,
   dried and halved
225 g/8 oz currants
225 g/8 oz raisins
225 g/8 oz sultanas
60 g/2 oz chopped candied lemon
   peel
60 g/2 oz chopped candied orange
   peel
115 g/4 oz blanched almonds, sliced
3 tablespoons brandy, plus
   2 tablespoons
285 g/10 oz plain flour
1 teaspoon salt
2 teaspoons mixed spice
225 g/8 oz butter
225 g/8 oz soft brown sugar
½ teaspoon vanilla essence
4 eggs, beaten
60 g/2 oz ground almonds

*This is my favourite Christmas
cake recipe. To give your cake time
to mature, make it at least four
weeks ahead. Then it will be ready
for icing the week before
Christmas. Always use the very
best fruit you can find: muscatel
raisins, undyed cherries, real
candied lemon and orange peel
and the freshest almonds.*

Mix the fruit and sliced almonds
together in a large bowl, pour over
3 tablespoons brandy, stir well and
set aside. Mix the flour, salt and
spice in a separate bowl and set
aside. Cream the butter with the
sugar and beat until light and
fluffy. Add the vanilla to the
beaten egg, and add this to the
butter mixture a little at a time.
You may need to add a little flour
with the last of the egg to prevent
the mixture curdling.

Fold the rest of the flour and
spice mixture into the butter along
with the ground almonds. Then
fold in the fruit, scraping in all the
brandy. Mix carefully until well
combined and spoon into a lined
20 cm/8 inch round cake tin. I
always tie a double layer of brown
paper around the outside of the tin
to prevent a hard crust forming
during the long cooking time. Bake
in a preheated oven at 150°C/
300°F/Gas 2 for 1½ hours, then
lower the heat to 140°C/275°F/
Gas 1 for a further 2½ hours.

The cake will be golden brown,
and when a tester is inserted in the
centre, it will come out clean. If
there is any trace of raw mixture
on the tester, continue to cook for
a further 20–30 minutes, and re-
test. If at any time the cake looks
as if it is becoming too brown on
top, cover with a double sheet of
greaseproof.

Once the cake is cooked, remove
from the oven and allow it to cool
in the tin. Remove the cake from
the tin, but leave it wrapped in the
greaseproof lining, and pour over
the last 2 tablespoons brandy.
Wrap the cake in a double layer of
aluminium foil, then store in an
airtight tin until needed.

ALADDIN CAKE

200 g/7 oz rich fruit cake (no icing)
110 g/4 oz butter
110 g/4 oz caster sugar
2 size 2 eggs
110 g/4 oz self-raising flour
1 teaspoon baking powder
grated rind and juice of a small
   orange
1 teaspoon demerara sugar

*If you have a small piece of
Christmas cake left over that no
one wants to eat, use it as the base
for a fresh cake.*

In a food processor reduce the
cake to crumbs.

Beat the butter and caster sugar
together until light and fluffy. Add
the eggs a little at a time and then
the flour, baking powder, orange
rind and juice and the cake
crumbs.

Spoon the mixture into a
buttered, floured 8 cm/7 inch cake
tin, sprinkle the top with demerara
sugar and bake in a preheated
oven at 180°C/350°F/Gas 5 for
40–50 minutes or until well risen
and pulling slightly from the sides
of the tin. A cake tester inserted in
the centre should come out clean.
Allow to cool for 10 minutes
before removing from the tin.
Finish cooling on a rack.

CHRISTMAS CRUMBLE CAKE

340 g/12 oz self-raising flour
1 teaspoon baking powder
½ teaspoon grated nutmeg
170 g/6 oz caster sugar
2 size 2 eggs
8 tablespoons milk
110 ml/4 fl oz vegetable oil
340 g/12 oz mincemeat

topping
30 g/1 oz butter
45 g/1½ oz plain flour
55 g/2 oz soft brown sugar
2 teaspoons cinnamon

Mix the flour, baking powder,
nutmeg and caster sugar together.
Beat the eggs with the milk and
oil and stir these into the dry
ingredients. Mix in the mincemeat
and spoon the mixture into a
greased 30 × 23 × 5 cm/12 × 9
× 2 inch tin.

Rub the topping ingredients
together until the mixture
resembles fine crumbs and sprinkle
these in an even layer over the
cake. Bake in a preheated oven at
190°C/375°F/Gas 5 for 40–50
minutes until well risen and
beginning to pull from the sides of
the tin. A cake tester inserted in
the centre should come out clean.
Allow to cool in the tin before
slicing into squares.

CHRISTMAS PUDDING

115 g/4 oz shredded suet
115 g/4 oz soft brown sugar
115 g/4 oz lexia raisins
115 g/4 oz chopped stoned prunes
60 g/2 oz candied peel
½ teaspoon mixed spice
¼ nutmeg, grated
115 g/4 oz two-day-old brown
  breadcrumbs
115 g/4 oz ground almonds
60 g/2 oz plain flour
60 g/2 oz blanched almonds,
  roughly chopped
115 g/4 oz glacé cherries
2 size 2 eggs
4 tablespoons milk
2 tablespoons brandy, plus
  2 tablespoons

Make your Christmas puddings
about six weeks before Christmas
to allow them to mature. This
recipe will make a 1.5 kg/3 lb
pudding that needs 4 hours boiling
on the day, and feeds 10–12
people, or two 725 g/1½ lb
puddings that need 2–3 hours
boiling and feed 5–6 each. Because
mine is to be a plum pudding I
have used prunes, but you may
prefer to substitute sultanas.

Mix all the dry ingredients
together. Beat together the egg,
milk and brandy and stir into the
dry ingredients. Mix well and leave
overnight in a cool place. Next
day, stir well, making sure all
members of the family take turns
to wish, and then fill one large or
two medium pudding basins.

Place two rounds of greaseproof
paper on the pudding mixture,
then cover the bowl with a double
layer of greaseproof, pleated down
the centre, and finally a double
layer of foil.

Tie the top layers on tightly with
string, looping the ends over to
make a handle. This will make it
possible for you to lift the pudding
from the hot water.

Cook the pudding in a saucepan,
or if more convenient a fish kettle,
filled two-thirds with hot water.
Keep the water simmering, topping
up as necessary for 6–8 hours.
While it is not strictly necessary to
cook the puddings for this long, it
does improve the colour and
flavour.

Allow the pudding to cool, then
remove the foil and top layer of
greaseproof. Pour the remaining
brandy around the edges of the
bowl so it can seep under the
circles of greaseproof, then recover
with fresh greaseproof and foil,
tying on as before. Store in a cool
dark place until needed. Small
coins, wrapped in foil, can be
inserted into the base of the
pudding with the tip of a sharp
knife just before it is turned out.

Mincemeat Cake

140 g/5 oz butter
115 g/4 oz caster sugar
3 medium eggs, beaten
200 g/7 oz self-raising flour
1 teaspoon baking powder
310 g/11 oz mincemeat
whole almonds to decorate

Quick to make at the last minute, this light, fruity cake has a very Christmassy flavour.

Cream the butter with the sugar until light and fluffy. Add the eggs a little at a time, alternating with a spoonful of the flour, sifted with the baking powder. Once all the egg has been added, fold in the remaining flour and the mincemeat.

Pour into a greased 20 cm/8 inch cake tin and decorate the top with almonds in a star pattern. Bake in a preheated oven at 180°C/360°F/ Gas 4 for 60–65 minutes. Allow to cool, then remove from the tin.

Last-Minute Christmas Pudding

170 g/6 oz wholemeal breadcrumbs
225 g/8 oz mixed dried fruit
(raisins, peel, sultanas etc.)
30 g/1 oz blanched almonds, chopped
85 g/3 oz dark brown sugar
2 tablespoons brandy
60 g/2 oz butter, melted
220 ml/8 fl oz milk
grated zest and juice of ½ lemon
1 size 2 egg, beaten
2 teaspoons mixed spice
½ teaspoon freshly grated nutmeg

This is not really a Christmas pudding but if you don't tell anyone, I'm sure they won't guess! You can mix the ingredients the night before and cook the pudding on the day.

Mix everything together well and put in a covered bowl in the fridge overnight. Butter a fluted cake tin and press the mixture in well.

Bake in a preheated oven at 180°C/360°F/Gas 4 for 1¼–1½ hours. Turn on to a heated serving dish and pour over a little extra brandy.

Serve with cream or brandy butter.

SUET-FREE CHRISTMAS PUDDING

500 g/1 lb 2 oz bag mixed fruit
60 g/2 oz ready-to-eat pitted
  prunes, chopped
115 g/4 oz dark muscovado sugar
150 ml/¼ pint stout
60 g/2 oz plain flour
115 g/4 oz white or brown
  breadcrumbs
115 g/4 oz frozen butter
60 g/2 oz ground almonds
2 teaspoons mixed spice
½ teaspoon freshly grated nutmeg
1 teaspoon ground cinnamon
85 g/3 oz chopped walnuts
85 g/3 oz chopped cherries
3 size 2 eggs, beaten
2 tablespoons dark rum

Necessity is the mother of invention and, having no suet in the house, I devised a Christmas pudding that's perfect for vegetarians. I also used a packet of ready mixed fruit to save having half empty bags of sultanas in the cupboards.

Put the mixed fruit, prunes, sugar, and stout into a bowl, stir well and leave overnight.

Place the flour and breadcrumbs in a large mixing bowl and coarsely grate in the frozen butter. Toss the butter flakes in the flour. Add the ground almonds, spices, walnuts and cherries, and then the fruit and any juice that has collected in the bowl. Now add the eggs and rum and mix thoroughly together. If the mixture is a little stiff add 1–2 tablespoons stout or milk. When all the family have had a stir and a wish, cover the bowl and leave in a cool place overnight.

Next day press the mixture into a greased 1.5 litre/2½ pint pudding bowl or two 600 ml/ 1 pint bowls, and cover with a double layer of greased paper and a double layer of pleated foil, tied on with string. Steam the pudding in a deep pan half filled with water for 8–9 hours. The smaller puddings take 4–5 hours. If you're cooking more than one pudding, try using a casserole dish or fish kettle instead of saucepans.

Remove the pudding from the pan, allow to cool, then cover with fresh paper and foil and store in a cool dry place until needed.

On Christmas Day steam the large pudding for 3 hours, the smaller ones for 2 hours, and serve with cream, whipped with a dash of brandy.

CHRISTMAS TRIFLE

1 packet/8 trifle sponges or a fatless
   18 cm/7 inch diameter sponge cake
100 ml/⅙ pint medium sherry
2–3 tablespoons raspberry or
   strawberry jam
4 medium bananas, sliced, or 1 jar
   fruit in brandy syrup
60 g/2 oz blanched almonds,
   roughly chopped

for the custard
8 cm/3 inch strip of vanilla pod
550 ml/1 pint single cream or
   creamy milk
3 egg yolks
1 tablespoon cornflour

to decorate
whipped cream
angelica
gold and silver dragées

Crumble the sponges into a glass
bowl and pour over the sherry. If
using fruit in brandy syrup, you
may use a little of this instead. Dot
the cake with jam and add the
sliced fruit and nuts.

Make the custard. Split the
vanilla pod and scrape out the tiny
black seeds. Stir these into the
cream and bring to just under
boiling point. Mix the egg yolks,
cornflour and sugar to a smooth
paste, add a little hot cream and
mix. Add the remaining cream,
then strain the mixture into a clean
saucepan and cook, stirring until it
thickens. Cook for 1–2 minutes
until no raw taste remains, then
pour the hot custard over the
sponge mixture and allow to set.

Decorate with whipped cream,
angelica and dragées.

CHRISTMAS PRUNE, ALMOND AND BRANDY TART

225 g/8 oz shortcrust pastry
225 g/8 oz dried prunes, soaked
   and drained, or 1 jar prunes in
   brandy (page 97)
275 ml/½ pint soured cream
3 egg yolks
60 g/2 oz caster sugar
60 g/2 oz ground almonds
45 g/1½ oz butter, melted
1 tablespoon brandy

Line a 23 cm/9 inch flan tin with
the pastry. Arrange the prunes on
the crust.

Beat the remaining ingredients
together well and pour over the
prunes. Bake in a preheated oven
at 190°C/375°F/Gas 5 for 30–40
minutes, until golden brown.

Serve warm. This pie may be
made ahead and reheated.

QUICK PRUNES IN BRANDY

225 g/8 oz dried prunes
cold tea
1 tablespoon brown sugar
brandy

These prunes may be used after 48 hours, but improve with keeping.

Cover the prunes with tea and soak overnight.

Add the sugar, bring to the boil and simmer gently for 2–3 minutes. Drain the prunes and transfer to a deep jar. Cover with brandy plus 2–3 tablespoons of the juice left in the saucepan.

Seal the jar and leave for as long as possible in a cool place.

KULISH
Russian Christmas bread

60 g/2 oz raisins
60 g/2 oz chopped mixed peel
1 tablespoon rum
285 g/10 oz plain flour
1 packet easy blend yeast
85 g/3 oz caster sugar
½ teaspoon salt
110 ml/4fl oz milk, warmed with a
  pinch of saffron
115 g/4 oz butter, melted
4 egg yolks, beaten
60 g/2 oz slivered almonds

to decorate
glacé icing
crystallized fruit

Soak the raisins and peel in the rum. In a large bowl mix the flour, yeast, sugar and salt. Add the remaining ingredients and mix well. Knead for about 5 minutes, cover and allow to rise until double in size.

Knock back the dough and knead for a further 2–3 minutes. Shape and put into a greased 900 g/2 lb loaf tin. Cover and leave to rise in a warm place for a further 30 minutes.

Bake in a preheated oven at 200°C/400°F/Gas 6 for 15 minutes, then continue to cook at 180°C/360°F/Gas 4 for 50 minutes, until well risen and golden brown.

Allow to cool on a rack before decorating. Pour thick glacé icing along the top of the loaf, allowing a little to run down the sides. Top with crystallized fruit.

CHRISTMAS LOAF

450 g/1 lb strong white bread flour
60 g/2 oz caster sugar
½ teaspoon salt
2 packets easy blend yeast
170 ml/6 fl oz warm milk or milk
   and water mixed
2 size 2 eggs, beaten
30 g/1 oz melted butter
1 teaspoon almond essence
60 g/2 oz chopped candied lemon
   peel
60 g/2 oz chopped candied orange
   peel
grated rind of 1 orange
grated rind of 1 lemon

to finish
225 g/8 oz ready made marzipan
beaten egg to glaze
thick glacé icing and slivered
   almonds, optional

I love to make special breads at Christmas and this one contains all my favourite things. The icing is optional. If left un-iced, the bread can be toasted carefully and served hot with butter.

Mix the flour, sugar, salt and yeast together well. Beat the milk, eggs, butter and essence into the flour and add the peels and rinds. Stir until you have a smoothish dough, then turn out on to a floured board and knead until the dough is light and elastic. The dough will be a little sticky, but add only enough flour to make it manageable.

Oil the outside of the dough, cover the bowl with a cloth and put to rise for about 2 hours until the dough has doubled in size.

Knock back and knead the dough lightly, then roll into an oblong about 30 × 20 cm/ 12 × 8 inches. Knead the marzipan until smooth then roll into a sausage about 30 cm/ 2 inches long. Place the marzipan sausage on the dough and roll the bread up to form a 30 cm/12 inch long loaf with the marzipan enclosed inside. Seal the ends well and place seam side down on a greased baking sheet. Re-cover with the cloth and put to rise again, this time for about 30 minutes, until double in size.

Brush the loaf with egg and bake in a preheated oven at 220°C/425°F/Gas 7 for 25–30 minutes or until the loaf sounds hollow when the base is tapped.

Allow to cool, then ice if desired and sprinkle liberally with slivered almonds.

SHORTBREAD WITH PINE NUTS

**115 g/4 oz butter or block
  margarine
170 g/6 oz plain flour
60 g/2 oz caster sugar
1 dessertspoon pine nuts
1 teaspoon demerara sugar**

*I've never quite understood why
Christmas sees a rush on to the
supermarket shelves of tins of
shortbread, as I love these rich
buttery biscuits at any time of the
year. However, homemade
shortbread does make a lovely
present packed in decorative boxes
or tins.*

Cut the butter into the flour, then
rub in well. Add the caster sugar
and continue to rub and work the
mixture until it forms a ball. You
can use a food processor to do
this.

Either roll out the ball into a
circle about 20 cm/8 inches across
and put on a baking sheet, pinch-
ing the edges to neaten them, or
press the mixture into a 20 cm/
8 inch square tin. Mark the shortbread into slices and decorate each
slice with a few pine nuts. Sprinkle
over the demerara sugar and bake
in a preheated oven at 190°C/375°F/
Gas 5 for 25 minutes on a baking
sheet, or 30 minutes in a tin.

Allow to cool, then cut into
slices along the guidelines. Store in
an airtight tin when cold.

Here are two variations on the
recipe.

For Walnut and cinnamon
shortbread: add 60 g/2 oz finely
ground walnuts and 1 teaspoon
cinnamon to the basic mixture,
then decorate with small pieces of
walnut.

For Wholemeal and orange
shortbread: use wholemeal instead
of plain flour, and soft brown
sugar instead of caster. Add the
grated rind of a small orange and
decorate with candied peel.

ALMOND PETTICOAT TAIL SHORTBREAD

140 g/5 oz plain flour
60 g/2 oz ground almonds
60 g/2 oz caster sugar
115 g/4 oz cold butter or block margarine

to finish
caster sugar
8 whole blanched almonds

This makes a delightful gift slipped on to a suitable plate, covered with cling film and decorated with a festive ribbon.

In a large bowl mix the flour, ground almonds and sugar. Cut the butter into small cubes, then rub it into the flour mixture. Keep working the crumbs until they begin to form a ball and finally knead for a few moments until you have a smooth dough.

Roll out a 20 cm/8 inch circle about 1 cm/½ inch thick and place carefully on a greased, floured baking sheet. Pinch and press the edges to neaten them, then mark the shortbread into 8 wedges. Lightly prick over with a fork, then sprinkle with a little caster sugar. Press an almond into each petticoat tail and bake in a preheated oven at 190°C/375°F/Gas 5 for 25 minutes or until lightly browned. Allow to cool on the tray, then remove and store in an airtight tin.

ATHOLL BROSE

8 heaped tablespoons porridge oats
300 ml/½ pint thick or single cream
3–4 tablespoons Scotch whisky
3–4 tablespoons heather honey

This is a Scottish pudding for New Year. Atholl brose was originally a mixture of soaked oatmeal and honey, strained and then added to a bottle of whisky. The resultant drink was said to fortify one and keep out the cold. Here the oatmeal is soaked in cream and eaten in very small portions. A few raspberries would be delicious served alongside.

Place the oats in a large clean frying pan and toast them over a medium heat until they change colour and give off a lovely nutty aroma. Pour the oats into a bowl and add the cream, stir well, then add whisky and honey to taste. Don't worry if it seems a bit sloppy at this stage. Give everything a good stir and put in the fridge for 2 hours.

The oats will swell to give a fairly stiff consistency, so if you like you can add a little more cream, whisky or honey at this stage. Serve spooned into small dishes.

Christmas Gingerbread Biscuits

1 teaspoon ginger
1 teaspoon cinnamon
½ teaspoon mixed spice
340 g/12 oz plain flour
30 g/1 oz butter
30 g/1 oz lard
60 g/2 oz soft brown sugar
3 tablespoons golden syrup
3 tablespoons black treacle
¾ teaspoon bicarbonate of soda
1 tablespoon boiling water
1 size 2 egg
icing and silver balls to decorate

Cut these gingerbread biscuits into Christmas shapes, and use them to trim the tree. Make a hole in each cookie before baking and cook for an extra 3–4 minutes.

When measuring syrup or treacle, warm the tin for a few moments so that the syrup flows freely, then take out the required amount with a tablespoon.

Sift the spices into the flour. Beat the fat with the sugar, syrup and treacle until well mixed. Mix the bicarbonate of soda with the water and add to the fat, again beating in well. Add the egg and then the flour, a little at a time. You will have a firm dough. Turn it out and knead gently, then allow to rest for 30 minutes.

Roll out the dough as thinly as possible and cut into Christmas shapes. Bake in a preheated oven at 180°C/360°F/Gas 4 for 10–15 minutes, until puffy and a slightly deeper brown than golden. Allow to cool on a rack.

To finish the biscuits in the traditional manner, pipe on a design in thick glacé icing and decorate with silver balls.

DECORATED CHRISTMAS BISCUITS

225 g/8 oz butter
200 g/7 oz caster sugar
2 eggs, beaten
1 tablespoon ground almonds
400 g/14 oz plain flour
1½ tablespoons baking powder
½ teaspoon salt
grated rind of 1 lemon

A delightful tradition in America is to give homemade Christmas biscuits to friends, neighbours and favourite teachers. Given a little help, cooking Christmas biscuits in a multitude of shapes can be an enjoyable way for children to pass those last few days of waiting. The fun really starts with decorating them.

Make a dough by creaming the butter with the sugar, adding the eggs and then the remaining ingredients. Knead lightly. The dough will be rather soft and sticky. Cover and put into the fridge for 1 hour.

Cut the dough into quarters. Reserve one quarter for thumb print biscuits and almond wreaths. Roll the other three quarters out thinly. With Christmas cutters, cut out festive shapes.

Cook on baking sheets in a preheated oven at 180°C/360°F/ Gas 4 for 7–10 minutes. They should be light brown.

To decorate, you can make up a thin icing with icing sugar and lemon juice and paint this on the hot biscuits as soon as they come out of the oven. This gives a lovely sharp taste and a glossy finish. The icing can be coloured: green for trees, yellow for stars etc.

Or, you can make up some pots of thick icing, colour with festive colours and ice the cooled biscuits, decorating with silver balls, sprinkles and edible paints. They are meant to be gaudy and no matter how sickly, children will love them.

Now take the remaining quarter of the dough and divide into balls just smaller than walnuts.

With half of these balls make thumb print biscuits by placing the ball on a baking sheet and making an indentation with your thumb in the middle. Fill this with raspberry jam and bake as above.

Use the other half of the balls to make almond wreaths. Roll the balls into 10 cm/4 inch sausages and bring the ends round to meet. Place a whole almond over the join, brush with a little beaten egg, and bake as above.

When you have finished you will have about 7 dozen assorted biscuits. Pack them in boxes or arrange them on Christmas paper plates and cover with cling film.

OREHOVA POTICA
walnut cake

450 g/1 lb white bread flour
60 g/2 oz caster sugar
2 packets easy blend yeast
½ teaspoon salt
170 ml/6 fl oz warm milk
2 size 2 eggs, beaten
30 g/1 oz butter, melted

for the filling
140 g/5 oz finely chopped walnuts
85 g/3 oz soft butter
85 g/3 oz soft brown sugar
1 teaspoon cinnamon

to finish
milk
60 g/2 oz icing sugar

Marjan Lesnik, Claridge's chef,
told me of this Yugoslav recipe for
a festive bread to celebrate the
New Year.

Mix together all the ingredients for the dough and knead well. Cover and put to rise for about 2 hours, until doubled in size. Knock back the dough and knead lightly.

Divide the dough into two equal pieces and roll each piece into an oblong about 30 × 20 cm/12 × 8 inches. Mix the filling ingredients together and divide between the dough, spreading to cover each piece.

Roll up the oblongs as tightly as possible to give two 30 cm/12 inch 'sausages'. Place these side by side, touching each other, on a greased baking sheet. Cover and leave to rise for about 40 minutes. Heat the oven to 220°C/425°F/Gas 7 and bake for 30–35 minutes, until well risen and golden brown. The bread should sound hollow when the base is tapped.

Remove from the oven and brush the top of the hot bread with milk. Sift over a generous covering of icing sugar.

BASIC PANCAKE BATTER

140 g/5 oz plain flour
3 size 2 eggs
330 ml/12 fl oz milk or milk and
 water mixed
a pinch of salt
butter for frying

This quantity of batter makes about 20 pancakes. They freeze well if interlayered with strips of greaseproof paper and packed in a polythene bag.

Making stacks of pancakes layered with different fillings is a wonderful way to use leftovers or feed friends who are vegetarians. Layer ratatouille, mushrooms in creamy sauce, grated cheese, vegetable curries or what you will and reheat the 'cake' in a moderate oven before serving.

Few things are less digestible than a heavy pancake, so a few rules need to be followed.

1 The batter must not be too thick: it should flow easily round the pan, giving only the lightest covering. Should you need to thin the batter, do so by adding water a little at a time until the correct consistency is achieved.

2 I have not found that resting the batter makes a substantial difference to the lightness of pancakes, but as batter tends to thicken as it rests you may need to thin it down.

3 To cook pancakes I use a 20 cm/8 inch heavy based frying pan that has been well seasoned and does not stick. A smaller nonstick omelette pan would do.

4 The pan must be hot so that the batter sets quickly. Preheat the pan for a few minutes before greasing to avoid the oil burning.

5 Pancakes must be cooked over a good heat and turned or tossed only once.

6 The first pancake is often a little heavy, so you may need to discard it.

Sift the flour into a deep bowl, make a well in the centre and break in the eggs. Beat the mixture with a balloon whisk, adding a little milk until you have a thick batter. Beat this well to remove any lumps, add the salt, then whisk in the remaining milk. Strain into a jug for use.

This can be made in a food processor by combining all the ingredients and processing until smooth.

Heat the pan for 2–3 minutes until hot, then brush with a little butter. Holding the pan in one hand and the jug of batter in the other, pour a thin stream of the batter into the pan. Swirl the batter around the pan and pour back any excess into the jug.

Replace the pan on the heat and cook the pancake until it is golden brown at the edges and bubbling off the pan in the centre.

Either flip the pancake over with a palette knife or slip it down towards the base of the pan, and toss it over with a flick of the wrist. Throw the pancake high enough for it to turn over before landing in the pan.

CHOCOLATE ALMOND MERINGUES

3 egg whites
170 g/6 oz caster sugar
30 g/1 oz ground almonds
30 g/1 oz plain chocolate, grated

for the chocolate cream
275 ml/½ pint double cream
85 g/3 oz plain chocolate, melted
   and cooled

Pipe these chocolate and almond meringues into heart shapes and sandwich them together with chocolate cream for a Valentine's Day treat.

Whisk the egg whites until very stiff, then whisk in the sugar a little at a time, and continue beating until the mixture is thick and glossy. Mix the almonds and chocolate and fold carefully into the meringue.

Fill a piping bag with a plain nozzle and pipe heart shapes about 5 cm/2 inches high on a greased baking sheet. Bake the meringue hearts in a preheated oven 100°C/ 200°F/Gas ¼ for about 1 hour, or until the meringues are crisp and dry but not coloured.

Remove from the oven, allow to cool for a few minutes on the trays, then finish cooling on a rack.

For the filling, beat the cream until floppy then beat in the chocolate. Allow to set slightly, then sandwich the hearts together with chocolate cream.

APRIL FISH

450 g/1 lb ready made puff pastry
1 size 2 egg, plus 1 yolk
85 g/3 oz butter
85 g/3 oz caster sugar
30 g/1 oz self-raising flour
85 g/3 oz ground almonds

Across the channel the first of April is April Fish Day, with children trying to pin paper fish, undetected, on to the backs of friends and the whole family eating this delicious frangipani 'fish'.

First make a paper template for your fish. . . .

Roll out the pastry and cut two fish shapes round the template. Place one 'fish' on a greased baking sheet. Roll the other fish lightly to make it slightly larger, and cut two air vents. If liked, these can be shaped like fins and you can decorate the fish with pastry scales and a currant eye.

Beat the egg with the yolk and reserve about 1 teaspoon to glaze the pastry. Cream the butter and sugar and add the beaten egg. Fold in the flour and almonds, then spread the mixture over the smaller fish to within 2 cm/¾ inch of the edge of the pastry. Dampen the edges and place the decorated fish on top, sealing the edges well.

Brush with the reserved egg mixed with a little sugar and bake in a preheated oven at 220°C/ 425°F/Gas 7 for 25–35 minutes, until the fish is golden brown and well risen.

Eat warm.

LENTEN BUNS

makes 12
**400 g/14 oz strong white bread
flour**
1 packet easy blend yeast
¼ teaspoon salt
45 g/1½ oz sugar
200 ml/7 fl oz warm milk
45 g/1½ oz butter, melted
1 size 2 egg, beaten

for the filling
100 ml/⅙ pint single cream
½ teaspoon vanilla essence
60 g/2 oz coarsely ground almonds
45 g/1½ oz caster sugar
**200 ml/⅓ pint thick cream,
whipped**

*These Swedish buns are usually
eaten on Shrove Tuesday, but like
our own hot cross buns, they have
become so popular that they are
now available for several months
each year.*

Mix all the ingredients for the buns together, reserving a little beaten egg for glazing, to give a slightly sticky dough. Turn this on to a floured board and knead well for about 5 minutes. Form into a ball, then place in a covered bowl. Put the dough to rise for about 1 hour, until doubled in size.

Knock back the dough and knead lightly. Divide into 12 pieces and knead each one into a roll. Place on a greased baking sheet, cover and put to rise again for about 40 minutes, until doubled in size.

Brush the rolls with beaten egg and bake in a preheated oven at 230°C/450°F/Gas 8 for 12–15 minutes, or until well risen and golden brown. Allow to cool on a rack.

Slice the tops from the buns and scrape out some of the crumbs. Put these in a bowl and pour on the cream, vanilla, almonds and sugar. Mash together well and divide this mixture between the buns. Spoon on some whipped cream and replace the tops.

HOT CROSS BUNS

makes 12
340 g/12 oz strong white flour
60 g/2 oz light muscovado sugar
2 teaspoons mixed spice
½ teaspoon grated nutmeg
½ teaspoon salt
2 packets easy blend yeast
60 g/2 oz sultanas
60 g/2 oz chopped mixed peel
170 ml/6 fl oz warm milk and water
  mixed
1 egg, beaten
60 g/2 oz butter, melted

to finish
flour
water
1 tablespoon sugar
1 tablespoon milk

With a well known high street store selling excellent hot cross buns, the time and trouble devoted to homemade buns must be rewarded with a good result. I have been experimenting with easy blend yeast and have finally come up with a recipe for buns that are richly fruited and fragrant with spice, while still being very light. The dough is sticky to handle but the extra liquid helps improve the action of the yeast.

Mix all the dry ingredients and the fruit in a large bowl. Then stir in the wet ingredients. With your hand, mix and knead the dough until everything is well combined. It will be sticky. Cover the bowl with a cloth and put in a warm place to rise for about 2 hours.

When the dough has doubled in size, knock it back and turn it out on to a floured board. Knead it again, using a little flour if necessary, until smooth, then divide the dough into 12 pieces and lightly knead each one into a round bun. Make sure the fruit is well tucked inside. Put the buns on a baking sheet and allow to rise again for 40–50 minutes until double in size.

Meanwhile, make a small piece of dough from flour and water, roll it out and cut narrow strips. Lay these in crosses on the buns, then bake in a preheated oven at 220°C/425°F/Gas 7 for 20–25 minutes. Take the buns out of the oven and brush them with glaze made by dissolving the sugar in the milk.

SIMNEL CAKE

200 g/7 oz plain flour
60 g/2 oz ground almonds
½ teaspoon baking powder
½ teaspoon grated nutmeg
170 g/6 oz butter
170 g/6 oz caster sugar
3 large eggs, beaten
grated rind and juice of ½ lemon
200 g/7 oz currants
200 g/7 oz sultanas
85 g/3 oz mixed peel, preferably
**   freshly cut candied lemon peel**
450 g/1 lb commercially made
**   marzipan**
apricot jam

Simnel cake, the traditional Mother's Day gift, is a lightly fruited cake delicately spiced with nutmeg. Decorate it with fresh or crystallized flowers or bake it for Easter and top with 11 marzipan apostles.

Commercially made marzipan tends to hold together better in this cake and allows you to avoid the use of raw eggs.

Sift the flour with the almonds, baking powder and spice. Cream together the butter and sugar until light and fluffy. Beat in the egg a little at a time, then beat in the lemon rind and juice. Add a little flour if the mixture begins to curdle. Fold in the remaining flour, then mix in the fruit. Make sure everything is lightly but well combined.

Line an 18 cm/7 inch cake tin. Take just over a third of the marzipan, and roll out an 18 cm/7 inch circle. Put half the cake mixture in the tin and lay the marzipan on top. Top with the remaining mixture and level the surface. Bake in a preheated oven at 160°C/325°F/Gas 3 for 1 hour, and then at 150°C/300°F/Gas 2 for a further hour, or until the cake is cooked. It should be firm to touch and mid brown. Skewer testing is not advised as the soft marzipan sticks to the skewer, giving a confusing result. Remove from the oven and allow to cool.

When cold, take the cake from the tin and brush the top with a little warm apricot jam. Knead the remaining marzipan until soft and roll out. Cut an 18 cm/7 inch circle and place this on top of the cake. If this is an Easter cake use the marzipan trimmings to make 11 small balls and place them in a circle round the cake. Preheat the grill and put the cake underneath, turning until the marzipan is just browned. For a Mother's Day cake fresh flowers, especially primroses, would look delightful.

SHREWSBURY BISCUITS

115 g/4 oz butter
115 g/4 oz caster sugar
1 medium egg, beaten
grated rind of 1 large lemon
225 g/8 oz flour
60 g/2 oz currants
1 teaspoon caraway seeds

These delicious lemon spice biscuits are an Easter tradition in 'Shrovesbury'. If you don't like the taste of caraway you can leave out the seeds.

Cream the butter and sugar together until light and fluffy, then beat in the egg and lemon rind. Now mix in the flour, currants and seeds. Form the mixture into a soft ball and put into the fridge for at least 1 hour.

As this dough is very soft it is important to work quickly. Use a floured board and chill the dough between rollings if necessary. Roll out the dough to about 5 mm/¼ inch thick, cut out the biscuits and then re-roll the dough until it is all used.

Place the biscuits on a baking sheet, sprinkle them with caster sugar and bake in a preheated oven at 180°C/360°F/Gas 4 for 15–20 minutes, until lightly browned.

EASTER NESTS

60 g/2 oz butter
2 tablespoons golden syrup
60 g/2 oz drinking chocolate powder
85 g/3 oz puffed rice cereal
small sugar eggs

Children love to make these as presents for friends.

Melt the butter with the syrup and stir in the chocolate powder, then mix in the cereal. Put spoonfuls into paper cake cases, forming into nest shapes and top with one or two sugar eggs. Allow to set in a cool place.

EASTER PIE

450 g/1 lb low fat cottage cheese
140 ml/¼ pint soured cream
170 g/6 oz caster sugar
3 eggs
rind and juice of 1 lemon
100 g/3½ oz blanched almonds
60 g/2 oz mixed peel
6–8 sheets filo dough
melted butter

This pie makes a spectacular finale to your Easter Sunday lunch.

In a food processor, mix the cottage cheese and soured cream until smooth, then add the sugar, eggs, lemon rind and juice, and the almonds. Process for 2–3 minutes to chop the almonds. (If you do not have a food processor use ground almonds.) Mix in the peel.

To prepare the pastry case, open the packet of filo and cover with a damp cloth as you work. Brush a 20 cm/8 inch springform tin with melted butter. Brush each sheet of filo well with butter and lay it in the tin with the edges hanging over the sides. Continue until you have an even lining.

Pour the filling into the case and gently fold over the pastry edges, giving a rough finish. Brush the top with melted butter and sprinkle with caster sugar.

Bake in a preheated oven at 180°C/360°F/Gas 4 for 55–65 minutes. The pie will be golden brown and crisp. Allow to cool and serve at room temperature.

MAZANEC

450 g/1 lb plain flour
2 sachets easy blend yeast
85 g/3 oz caster sugar
½ teaspoon salt
grated rind of 1 large lemon
85 g/3 oz raisins
60 g/2 oz slivered almonds
140 g/5 oz melted butter
220 ml/8 fl oz warm milk
4 egg yolks, beaten
1 teaspoon vanilla essence

to finish
beaten egg to glaze
30 g/1 oz slivered almonds

Mazanec and Venec (see page 111) are both yeast breads from Czechoslovakia, and are traditionally eaten at Eastertide. Mazanec is shaped like a huge bun and marked with a cross.

Mix the flour, yeast, sugar, salt, lemon rind, raisins and almonds in a bowl. Add the remaining ingredients and beat well with a spoon. Cover and leave to rise in a warm place for about 2 hours, until doubled in size. Turn out on to a well floured board and knead lightly. The dough will be sticky.

Shape into a large round bun and place on a greased baking sheet, cover and leave to rise again until doubled in size. Brush with beaten egg and sprinkle with almonds. With a very sharp knife, cut a cross on the top.

Bake in a preheated oven at 200°C/400°F/Gas 6 for 35–40 minutes, or until well risen and golden brown. Allow to cool on a rack.

Venec

450 g/1 lb plain flour
1 packet easy blend yeast
30 g/1 oz caster sugar
1 teaspoon salt
grated rind of 1 lemon
60 g/2 oz butter, melted, plus
**   45 g/1½ oz soft butter**
2 egg yolks plus 1 egg, beaten
**   together**
170 ml/6 fl oz single cream,
**   warmed**

to finish
beaten egg to glaze
30 g/1 oz slivered almonds

Another Easter yeast bread from Czechoslovakia, Venec is a wonderfully elaborate woven crown to fill with coloured eggs.

Place the dry ingredients in a large bowl and mix in the melted butter, eggs and cream. Turn out on to a lightly floured board and knead for 8–10 minutes.

Replace the dough in the bowl and allow to rise for about 2 hours, until double in size. Knock back the dough and knead lightly. Roll the dough until you have a large rectangle and spread this with the softened butter. Fold up as for puff pastry, top third down, bottom third up. Give the dough a quarter turn and roll out again. Repeat this folding and rolling twice more.

Divide the rectangle of dough into five strips, take three of these, and squeeze and pull them into long ropes. Plait the ropes. The plait should be about 51 cm/20 inches long. Form it into a circle on a baking sheet. Pinch the ends together well and brush with egg.

Take the remaining pieces of dough and twist them together to form a rope. Make a circle with this and lay it on top of the plait. Pinch the ends together well.

Cover with a damp cloth and leave to rise until double in size. Glaze with the remaining egg and sprinkle with almonds. Bake the loaf in a preheated oven at 200°C/400°F/Gas 6 for 50–60 minutes, or until glossy and golden brown.

Allow to cool, then tie with a green ribbon and fill with decorated eggs.

FLOATING ISLANDS

420 ml/¾ pint single cream
5 cm/2 inch piece vanilla pod or
½ teaspoon vanilla essence
3 size 2 eggs, separated
2 tablespoons caster sugar
2 tablespoons orange liqueur
115 g/4 oz caster sugar
crystallized rose and violet petals
to decorate

This is another perfect dessert to eat on Easter Sunday.

Start by making the custard. Heat the cream to boiling point. Split open the vanilla pod and scrape out the tiny black seeds, then stir these into the hot cream. Mix the egg yolks with the 2 tablespoons sugar and then add the scalded cream. Strain the mixture back into the saucepan and, over a very low heat and stirring constantly, cook the custard until it just coats the back of a spoon. It must not boil.

Strain the custard again and add the liqueur. Pour into a serving dish, cover with cling film, and put into the fridge.

Whisk the egg whites until stiff, then beat in the remaining sugar. Continue to beat the mixture until stiff and glossy.

Set a deep frying pan on the stove with about 4 cm/1½ inches boiling water and allow to simmer. The water should just tremble.

Using two dessert spoons, shape 'islands' of meringue and gently drop them into the water. Poach the islands, 4 or 5 at a time, for 60 seconds, then turn and cook the other side for a further 60 seconds. Remove from the water and drain on a folded tea towel.

When they are all cooked carefully float them on the custard and at the last moment sprinkle on the crystallized flowers.

CHAPTER
6
Puddings

THE SUBJECT OF this final chapter is closest to many people's hearts. The idea of pudding, and even the word itself, is wonderfully comforting. No one actually needs to eat pudding: it is pure self-indulgence and luxury designed to soothe the spirit in a less than perfect world.

About two years ago I stopped at a pub for lunch when driving through the country. It was a very grand pub, more of a coaching inn in fact, and the packed dining room was unusually quiet. It took a moment before I realized that all the diners were tucking into large dishes of steaming spotted dick and custard. Not a word was said: all I could hear was the steady sound of eating and the odd contented sigh.

There are few dishes to beat an old-fashioned British steamed pudding on a cold day, but this chapter also offers some new surprises – how about lemon meringue rice pudding, and hot chocolate soufflé? Hot puddings begin on page 136.

But first the cold puddings. Did you know that Alexander the Great brought down snow from the glaciers and mixed it with fruit pulp and wine to refresh his thirsty troops? Ices have remained popular ever since, and I include several recipes here in a wide selection ranging from a simple meringue to a sophisticated Charlotte Russe.

SUMMER PUDDING

6–8 slices wholemeal bread
725 g/1½ lb assorted red summer
fruit: rhubarb, black and red
currants, raspberries,
strawberries
115 g/4 oz caster sugar, or to taste

I like to make summer pudding
with brown bread and as wide a
selection of summer fruits as
possible

Lightly brush a 900 ml/1½ pint
basin with oil. Cut the crusts from
the bread and use the slices to line
the bowl. Press the seams together
well. You should have sufficient
bread left over for a lid.

Put into a saucepan the fruit that
will take longest to cook, such as
rhubarb, and black and red
currants, and add caster sugar.
Poach the fruit until the juices run
and the fruit is tender.

Then add the raspberries and
sliced large or whole small
strawberries. Check the sweetness,
adding more sugar if needed. Pour
the fruit mixture and all the juice
into the bread-lined basin, filling as
full as possible.

Arrange the bread slices, cut as
necessary, to form a lid over the
fruit, cover with cling film and
then with a weighted plate. Leave
at least 6 hours and preferably
overnight before turning out.

Serve with cream.

WINTER FRUIT SALAD

60 g/2 oz each dried apple rings,
peaches, pears, prunes, apricots,
figs
3–4 tablespoons dark muscovado
sugar
10 cm/4 inches cinnamon stick
1 long curl lemon peel

This recipe comes from a very
good friend who lives in Norfolk.

Place the fruit in a deep bowl, pour
on water and leave overnight to
soak. Put the fruit, soaking water,
sugar, cinnamon and lemon peel
into a saucepan and bring to the
boil. Simmer for 20–30 minutes or
until cooked to taste. Serve hot or
cold with Dairy mallow, below.

DAIRY MALLOW

420 ml/¾ pint natural yogurt
275 ml/½ pint whipped cream
demerara sugar

Another recipe from my Norfolk friend.

Fold the yogurt into the whipped cream and spoon a third of the mixture into a glass serving bowl. Sprinkle on a thin layer of demerara sugar and then add another layer of yogurt and cream. Continue until all the cream is used and finish with a layer of sugar. Refrigerate overnight and serve with winter fruit salad, above.

ORANGES IN CARAMEL GINGER SYRUP
with cardamom cream

6 medium oranges
3 pieces stem ginger in syrup
60 g/2 oz caster sugar
140 ml/¼ pint water
3 tablespoons syrup from ginger
4–6 cardamom pods
275 ml/½ pint double cream
sugar to taste

With a sharp knife, cut the peel and pith from the oranges. Slice them into a glass serving dish and add the stem ginger cut into fine matchsticks. In a heavy bottomed saucepan melt the sugar and cook, stirring often, until it caramelizes.

When the caramel is mid-brown, remove the pan from the heat and very carefully, at arm's length, add the water. The caramel will bubble up. Stir to dissolve any lumps in the syrup, heating if necessary. Allow the syrup to cool, add the ginger syrup and pour over the fruit. Refrigerate until needed.

To prepare the cream, take the seeds from the cardamom pods and crush them. Beat the cream until thick, adding sugar to taste, then the cardamom. Hand round with the oranges.

ROSE SCENTED RHUBARB FOOL

725 g/1½ lb rhubarb
60 g/2 oz sugar, or to taste
275 ml/½ pint double cream
140 ml/¼ pint thick Greek yogurt
1-2 tablespoons rosewater

This dessert looks wonderful served in small glass dishes decorated with pale pink rose petals.

Wash the rhubarb and slice into a saucepan with the sugar. It is important not to add too much liquid at this stage, so cook the rhubarb very slowly with the sugar and the water that clings to it. Once the rhubarb has given out its juice, simmer for 4–6 minutes, until very soft. Allow to cool.

Whip the cream until it begins to thicken, add the yogurt and continue to beat until quite stiff but not solid. Fold in the rhubarb with the rosewater until just combined, then chill.

SOUP OF THE RED FRUITS

½ bottle red wine (Cabernet Sauvignon)
1.15 kg/2½ lb assorted red fruit, such as redcurrants, blueberries, blackberries, blackcurrants, raspberries, cherries, strawberries
170 g/6 oz sugar, to taste

This delicious French dessert is quick to make and keeps well in the fridge. Serve with cream, Greek yogurt or blackcurrant sorbet. If possible, use at least four types of berries, mixing frozen with fresh as available.

Put the wine into a large saucepan and add all the fruit that needs cooking: currants, blackberries, blueberries and cherries.

Dissolve the sugar in the mixture and allow it to barely simmer for 4–5 minutes. Remove from the heat and let it cool, then add the strawberries and raspberries. Pour into a glass serving bowl and refrigerate until needed.

PAIN PERDU
with fresh fruit sauce

2 medium eggs
150 ml/¼ pint creamy milk
1–2 slices day-old French bread per person
oil for frying

for the sauce
45 g/1½ oz butter
45 g/1½ oz sugar
150 ml/¼ pint fresh orange juice
4 nectarines or peaches, sliced, or 340 g/12 oz strawberries or blackberries

Beat the egg with the milk and soak the bread in the mixture. Fry the soaked slices in a little oil a few at a time until golden on both sides. Keep warm.

For the sauce, melt the butter in a shallow pan, add the sugar and juice and stir until dissolved. Bring to the boil and simmer for 2 minutes. Add the sliced fruit, and cook for a minute or so until tender. (Strawberries will need only a few moments.)

Serve the sauce spooned over the fried bread slices.

PEACHES POACHED IN WHITE WINE

10–12 small peaches
115 g/4 oz caster sugar
400 ml/⅔ pint water
200 ml/⅓ pint white wine
1 cinnamon stick
raspberries, optional

Plastic punnets of peaches are now widely available in summer but the fruit are often underripe and shrivel quickly. Try poaching them in a white wine syrup to maximize their flavour.

In a saucepan large enough to take all the peaches heat the sugar and water, stirring until the sugar dissolves. Add the white wine, cinnamon stick and peaches, then simmer the fruit for 10 minutes or until a skewer slips easily into a peach.

Remove the fruit from the syrup and allow to cool for a few moments. Boil the syrup rapidly until reduced by one third. When the peaches are cool enough to touch, peel off the skins and return to the syrup.

Add a punnet of raspberries if available, and chill until needed.

SPICED PEARS IN RED WINE
with caramelized almonds

115 g/4 oz caster sugar
415 ml/¾ pint water
1 cinnamon stick
1 cm/½ inch root ginger, peeled
and chopped
4–6 large pears
140 ml/¼ pint red wine

to finish
1 teaspoon butter
1 teaspoon sugar
30 g/1 oz slivered almonds
thick cream or yogurt

Put the sugar and water into a medium saucepan and heat, stirring, until the sugar has dissolved, then add the cinnamon and ginger. Simmer, uncovered, for 5 minutes.

Peel the pears, slice in half and remove the cores. Lay in an ovenproof dish. Mix the wine into the spiced syrup and pour over the pears. For best results the pears should be completely submerged. Bake in a preheated oven at 150°C/300°F/Gas 2 for about 1 hour, or until tender. Remove from the oven and allow to cool.

To finish, melt the butter in a small frying pan and add the sugar, stir well, then add the almonds. Cook over a medium heat, stirring, until the almonds colour and the sugar caramelizes. Remove from the heat and tip on to a plate to cool.

Serve the pears in individual glass dishes topped with a spoonful of thick cream or Greek yogurt and sprinkled with the almonds.

GRAPE BRÛLÉE

725 g/1½ lb seedless grapes (or
frozen raspberries, chopped
peaches etc.)
275 ml/½ pint double cream
140 ml/¼ pint soured cream
dark muscovado sugar

Simplicity itself, this pudding needs to set overnight in the fridge before you caramelize the sugar topping.

Wash the grapes and drain well. Slice each grape in half and place in a shallow ovenproof dish. Beat the cream until stiff and fold in the soured cream. Spread this mixture carefully over the grapes, smoothing the top as much as possible. Refrigerate overnight.

Fifteen minutes before you are ready to finish the pudding, put the grill on to heat at its highest setting.

Carefully sprinkle a layer of sugar over the top of the cream, as smoothly and evenly as possible. Place the dish under the grill about 5 cm/2 inches below the element and, watching very carefully, heat until the sugar caramelizes. This will take 3–5 minutes. Too much cooking will cause the cream to boil and the sugar to burn.

Allow to cool before serving.

Fresh melon sorbet

1 ripe melon
juice of ½ lemon
icing sugar to taste

The flavour of this sorbet depends on the right choice of melon. Look for a ripe, orange fleshed melon such as Charentais, with a rich musky perfume.

Peel and deseed the melon. Place the flesh in a food processor and purée until very smooth. Add the lemon juice and sugar to taste. Pour the purée into a freezing tray or ice cream machine and freeze in the usual manner, breaking up the ice crystals with a fork twice if freezing in a tray.

Allow the sorbet to thaw for 20 minutes in the fridge before serving with cubes of watermelon or small biscuits.

Lemon ice cream

8 egg yolks
225 g/8 oz caster sugar
300 ml/½ pint thick double cream
juice and grated rind of 2 lemons

Using a hand held electric mixer, beat the yolks with the sugar over a saucepan of simmering water until the sugar has dissolved and you have a light thick mousse. Remove from the heat and allow to cool while you whip the cream with the lemon juice and rind. The cream should thicken to soft peak. Fold this into the egg mousse and turn into a suitable container for freezing.

Freeze in the coldest part of your freezer for at least 8 hours. This ice cream is very rich, so small portions are sufficient.

FRESH PINEAPPLE ICE

**1 ripe pineapple
juice of 1 large lemon
60 g/2 oz sugar, or to taste**

Cut the peel, core and eyes from the pineapple and liquidize in a food processor. Add the lemon juice and sugar to taste. Pour into a suitable container and freeze, stirring from time to time to break up the ice crystals.

Allow the ice to sit in the refrigerator for about 20 minutes, then serve with ginger biscuits (page 52).

BROWN BREAD ICE CREAM

**30 g/1 oz butter
30 g/1 oz soft brown sugar
85 g/3 oz brown breadcrumbs
600 ml/1 pint double cream
2–3 tablespoons caster sugar
1 teaspoon vanilla extract
1 tablespoon orange brandy,
    optional**

This is a delicious rich ice cream made without using raw eggs.

Melt the butter in a saucepan, then add the sugar and crumbs. Stir together well and spread the mixture on a baking sheet. Bake in a preheated oven at 180°C/360°F/ Gas 4, until crisp and browned. You will need to break up the lumps several times during cooking. Allow the crumbs to cool.

Beat the cream until it begins to thicken, then add sugar to taste. Continue to beat, adding the vanilla and orange brandy. The cream should be thick enough to hold its shape but not solid. Turn the cream into a freezing container and place in the freezer. Stir the ice cream 2 or 3 times as it freezes, to break up any ice crystals. Just before it is quite solid, stir in the cold crumbs. Freeze until solid.

STRAWBERRY YOGURT ICE

450 g/1 lb ripe strawberries, hulled
  and washed
115 g/4 oz icing sugar
1 tablespoon lemon juice
1 sachet gelatine
225 g/8 oz Greek yogurt

*Using yogurt instead of double
cream gives this strawberry ice a
light refreshing flavour.*

Process the strawberries with the
icing sugar and lemon juice in a
blender or food processor until
you have a smooth purée. Sprinkle
the gelatine over 3 tablespoons
warm water and leave to swell.
Add the yogurt to the fruit purée
in the blender and process to mix
well. Warm the gelatine and water
until the gelatine has dissolved,
then add to the fruit mixture,
again processing well.

Tip the mixture into a plastic
freezing tray and place in the quick
freeze zone of your freezer. When
the ice is beginning to solidify,
scrape it into the food processor
and mix for 60 seconds to break
up the ice crystals. Return to the
freezer at once and freeze until
hard.

Always allow homemade ices to
sit in the fridge for 20 minutes
before serving so they soften and
the flavour develops.

MANGO AND LEMON MOUSSE

2 ripe mangoes
grated rind and juice of 1 lemon
1 sachet gelatine
3 egg whites
60 g/2 oz caster sugar

*This fresh mango mousse is made
without cream, so is featherlight
and refreshing.*

Carefully cut all the flesh from the
mangoes, scraping as much as
possible from the stone without
including too many fibres. Scrub
the lemon under hot water, then
finely grate the rind. Put the
mango flesh, lemon rind and juice
into a processor or blender and
whizz until you have a smooth
purée.

Sprinkle the gelatine powder
over 3 tablespoons warm water
and leave to swell. Stand the bowl
in a pan of warm water and stir
until the powder has completely
dissolved. Mix this into the mango
purée, then pour the mixture into a
bowl and put in the fridge.

When the purée is beginning to
set, remove from the fridge. Beat
the egg whites to a light foam, add
the sugar, and continue to beat
until stiff and glossy. Carefully but
thoroughly fold the mango into the
egg whites with a metal spoon,
then pour into a fluted mould and
put in the fridge to set.

When ready to serve, dip the
mould into hot water for 20
seconds and turn out.

CHARLOTTE RUSSE

⅓ tablet lemon or lime jelly
1 packet/14–16 sponge fingers
angelica
cherries
1 sachet gelatine
415 ml/¾ pint double cream
sugar to taste
almond essence
brandy

Excellent for entertaining. Usually made with a bavarois filling, but I use liqueur-flavoured double cream set with gelatine.

Make the jelly with 200 ml/⅓ pint hot water and allow to cool. Pour a thin layer into the bottom of a charlotte mould and put in the fridge to set.

Dip each finger in the still liquid jelly and arrange around the edge of the charlotte mould. Carefully pour in a little more jelly, and put to set.

Arrange thin slices of angelica and cherries on the jelly in an attractive pattern. Cover with jelly and allow to set.

Sprinkle the gelatine on to 5 tablespoons warm water and put to swell. Beat the cream until floppy, sweeten, and add almond essence and brandy to taste.

Warm the gelatine gently to dissolve, then stir into the cream and fill the russe with the mixture. Level it off, cover with foil and put to set in the fridge.

This dessert can be frozen for 3–4 weeks. Defrost in the fridge overnight, then turn out on to a plate to serve.

CHOCOLATE CHESTNUT MOUSSE CAKE

100 g/3½ oz plain chocolate
115 g/4 oz soft butter
115 g/4 oz caster sugar
3 size 2 eggs, separated
2 tablespoons brandy
225 g/8 oz chestnut purée (tinned)

to serve
grated chocolate
marrons glacés
whipped cream

This chocolate chestnut cake is wonderfully rich, a perfect special occasion pudding.

Melt the chocolate in a bowl over a pan of boiling water, then allow to cool for 5 minutes.

Beat the butter and sugar together until light and fluffy. Add the egg yolks, brandy, chocolate and chestnut purée, and beat well. Whisk the whites to a snow. Do not overbeat: the whites should be stiff but not dry.

Fold the chocolate mixture into the egg whites and pour the batter into a lined, well greased, shallow 20 cm/8 inch cake tin. Bake in a preheated oven at 190°C/375°F/ Gas 5 for 35–45 minutes, until well risen and almost firm to the touch. The cake will still be a little soft in the middle. Remove from the oven and allow to cool. The cake will sink down. Turn it on to a serving plate, top with whipped cream and decorate with grated chocolate or marrons glacés.

CHOCOLATE AND CHESTNUT BOMBE

1 tin chestnut purée (no added
    sugar or salt)
1 teaspoon vanilla essence
115 g/4 oz icing sugar
1 tablespoon brandy, optional
415 ml/¾ pint double cream
70 g/2½ oz chocolate, grated

This could be the world's simplest chestnut pudding.

In a bowl beat the chestnut with the vanilla and sugar until the mixture is smooth and the sugar has dissolved. Check for sweetness. Remember that the dessert will be eaten frozen, so at this stage it should be quite sweet. Add the brandy if desired.

In a separate bowl beat the cream until floppy. Fold the chestnut mixture and all but 15 g/ ½ oz of the chocolate into the cream until well combined. Be careful, as the mixture thickens quite quickly. Put the remaining chocolate into a 1 litre/2 pint pudding basin, then spoon the chestnut cream in on top. Press down well, cover the cream with a circle of greaseproof, then cover the dish firmly with cling film.

Place in the freezer and freeze overnight or until solid.

To serve, allow to sit in the fridge for about 15 minutes before needed, then turn out on to a serving plate, allowing the chocolate flakes to fall down over the bombe.

LEMON CHIFFON PIE
in a chocolate coconut shell

115 g/4 oz plain chocolate
60 g/2 oz butter
225 g/8 oz desiccated coconut

for the filling
3 eggs, separated
140 g/5 oz caster sugar
juice and rind of 2 lemons
1 sachet gelatine
300 ml/½ pint whipping cream

Carefully melt the chocolate with the butter. Stir in the coconut and press this over the base and sides of a 23 cm/9 inch springform tin. Put in the fridge for about 2 hours to set.

In a heavy saucepan beat the egg yolks and sugar together with the lemon juice. Put the mixture over a very low heat and whisk until thick and doubled in volume (do not allow to boil). Dissolve the gelatine in 2 tablespoons warm water, and whisk this into the egg and lemon mixture. Leave to cool.

When the mousse is cool and beginning to set, whisk the cream until thickened and the egg whites until stiff. Fold the cream, and then the whites into the lemon mixture and pour the filling into the coconut shell.

Allow the pie to set in the fridge for 2 hours.

LEMON MOUSSE
in a ginger shell

310 g/11 oz gingernut biscuits
85 g/3 oz butter, melted
1 sachet gelatine
3 size 2 eggs, separated
170 g/6 oz caster sugar
rind and juice of 2 lemons

This dessert looks lovely decorated with fresh flowers.

Crush the biscuits to fine crumbs and stir in the melted butter. Press this mixture into a loose bottomed 20 cm/8 inch cake tin, bringing the mixture as far up the sides as possible. Place in the fridge to cool.

Sprinkle the gelatine over 4 tablespoons warm water and allow to swell. Heat gently to dissolve the gelatine, then allow to cool.

Using an electric mixer, beat the egg yolks with the sugar, lemon rind and juice, until you have a thick pale mousse. Stir in the cooled gelatine mixture.

Whisk the egg whites until stiff and fold carefully into the setting lemon mousse. Pour into the ginger shell and allow to set in the fridge.

Remove from the tin to serve.

CRÈME BRÛLÉE 1

serves 6
550 ml/1 pint double cream
1 vanilla pod
6 egg yolks
60 g/2 oz caster sugar

for the topping
demerara or granulated sugar

Scald the cream with the vanilla pod, then remove the pod. (You can wash the pod and use it again.) Mix the egg yolks with the caster sugar until well blended, then pour in the hot cream.

Strain the mixture into 6 ramekin dishes and stand these in a baking tin half filled with cold water. Place the tin in a preheated oven at 150°C/300°F/Gas 2 and cook for 1 hour.

Remove the custards from the oven and from the tin of water and allow to cool. Store overnight in the fridge.

About an hour before needed, make the caramel topping. The traditional method is to sprinkle the tops of the custards to cover completely with demerara sugar, then melt the sugar under a very hot grill. I find it much easier to melt very carefully in a saucepan 2 tablespoons granulated sugar per ramekin, and then pour the resulting caramel over the tops of the custards, and allow it to set.

Serve the crèmes brûlées with a bowl of fresh raspberries.

CRÈME BRÛLÉE 2

serves 4
140 ml/¼ pint single cream
415 ml/¾ pint double cream
1 vanilla pod
5 egg yolks
70 g/2½ oz caster sugar
**1 small chunk plain chocolate,
    grated**

to finish
preserving sugar

Scald the creams with the vanilla pod and leave to infuse for 15 minutes.

Whisk the egg yolks with the sugar, then whisk in the hot cream. Strain the mixture into 4 wide soup bowls, sprinkle the tops with a little grated chocolate and bake in a water bath (as for the previous recipe) at 150°C/300°F/Gas 2 for 20–25 minutes until set.

Allow to cool and cover each dish with cling film. Chill.

To serve, coat the surface of the custard generously with preserving sugar. Heat the grill for 10–15 minutes until very hot. Place the bowls under the grill, watching carefully, until the sugar caramelizes. Remove, allow to cool and serve.

ICE CREAM-FILLED CHOUX PUFFS
with raspberry sauce

vanilla ice cream
icing sugar
340 g/12 oz raspberries

for the choux paste
140 ml/¼ pint water
60 g/2 oz butter
70 g/2½ oz plain flour
2 size 3 eggs, beaten

Put the water and butter in a nonstick pan and heat until the butter has melted. Bring to the boil and add the flour all at once. Remove from the heat and beat well with a wooden spoon. The mixture should form a smooth ball. Allow this to cool for a few minutes, then beat in the egg a little at a time.

Put tablespoonfuls of this glossy mixture on a damp baking sheet and bake in a preheated oven at 200°C/400°F/Gas 6 for 10 minutes, then turn down the heat and bake at 160°C/325°F/Gas 3 for a further 15–20 minutes, or until puffy and golden brown. Allow to cool on a rack.

When cold, split open the puffs and remove any soft pastry from the inside. Fill the puffs with ice cream and dust with icing sugar. To make the sauce, rub the raspberries through a sieve and sweeten with icing sugar to taste.

Serve the puffs with the sauce.

Rum baba

makes 8–10
150 ml/¼ pint warm milk
1 packet easy blend yeast
340 g/12 oz plain flour
2 tablespoons caster sugar
1 teaspoon salt
4 size 3 eggs, beaten
115 g/4 oz butter, melted
60 g/2 oz raisins

for the syrup
225 g/8 oz caster sugar
450 ml/¾ pint water
rum to taste

Mix all the dough ingredients except the butter and raisins in a bowl and beat well with a wooden spoon. Cover the bowl and put to rise in a warm place. When the dough has doubled in size, beat in the butter and raisins, mixing well. Spoon the mixture into greased individual tart tins, dariole moulds or deep bun tins, filling them about half full. Allow the dough to rise until just level with the top of the tins, then bake in a preheated oven at 220°C/425°F/Gas 7 for 15–20 minutes, until golden brown.

Meanwhile, make the syrup: dissolve the sugar in the water and boil for 5 minutes. Remove from the heat and allow to cool a little, then add rum to taste.

Remove the babas from the oven, allow them to cool for 5 minutes, then take them from their tins and arrange in a single layer in a large dish. Pour the warm syrup over the warm babas, basting with any that runs into the dish. Allow to cool and serve with cream.

Vanilla rice cream
with strawberries

60 g/2 oz short grain rice
550 ml/1 pint milk
5 cm/2 inch piece vanilla pod
2 egg yolks
3–4 tablespoons caster sugar
1 packet gelatine
140 ml/¼ pint whipping cream

to serve
strawberries, sliced

Wash the rice well under cold running water, then place with the milk and vanilla pod in a heavy bottomed saucepan. Bring to the boil and simmer, stirring occasionally, for 25–30 minutes, or until the rice is tender. The mixture should be creamy but not dry. Remove from the heat and allow to cool slightly.

Remove the vanilla pod, squeeze out the seeds and return them to the rice. Discard the pod. Stir in the egg yolks and sugar to taste.

Sprinkle the gelatine over 3 tablespoons water and allow to swell. Warm gently until the powder has completely dissolved, then stir into the rice mixture. Allow to cool until just beginning to set.

Whip the cream until floppy and stir into the setting rice. Pour into a fluted mould or bowl, and place in the fridge to set.

To serve, place the mould in a bowl of very hot water for 15 seconds, then invert on to a serving dish. Pile the strawberries around the base, sprinkling on a little caster sugar if you like.

APRICOT FOOL

225 g/8 oz dried apricots
1 sachet gelatine
juice of ½ lemon
150 ml/¼ pint soured cream
2–3 tablespoons caster sugar
2 egg whites

Cover the apricots well with water and soak overnight. Place the soaked fruit and about 450 ml/¾ pint of the soaking water in a pan and bring to the boil. Simmer the fruit until tender. Pour the fruit and liquid into a food processor or blender and sprinkle on the gelatine. Process the mixture for 3–4 minutes until smooth.

Add the lemon juice, cream and sugar to taste and pour into a bowl. Allow to cool until just beginning to set, then whisk the egg whites to a firm snow and fold in thoroughly. Pour into a serving bowl and place in the fridge until set.

ALMOND CREAM
with red fruit compote

100 g/3½ oz blanched almonds
1 sachet gelatine
275 ml/½ pint milk
3 egg yolks
60 g/2 oz caster sugar
1 teaspoon cornflour
½ teaspoon almond essence
275 ml/½ pint whipping cream
450 g/1 lb red and black currants
sugar to taste

Chop the almonds finely in a food processor or coffee mill. Sprinkle the gelatine on 6 tablespoons water and allow to swell. Scald the milk briefly.

Mix the egg yolks with the sugar and the cornflour and add the milk. Pour the mixture back into the saucepan and stir the custard constantly until it thickens, is just at boiling point and coats the back of the spoon. Check no raw taste remains.

Strain the custard into a bowl, add the almonds, the essence and the gelatine, stirring until the gelatine has dissolved. Leave to cool. Just before the almond custard sets, beat the cream and fold in. Pour into a fluted mould.

Gently cook the prepared currants with sugar to taste. Allow to cool. Just before serving, dip the mould into boiling water for 15 seconds and invert on to a plate. Serve with the currant compote.

LEMON AND FROMAGE FRAIS MOUSSE

rind and juice of 2 lemons
1 packet gelatine
2 size 2 eggs, separated
140 g/5 oz caster sugar
225 g/8 oz 8% fat fromage frais

Dilute half the lemon juice with 1 tablespoon water and sprinkle over the gelatine powder.

Using an electric mixer beat the egg yolks with the lemon rind, the remaining juice and half the caster sugar, until you have a thick pale mousse. Warm the gelatine until it has dissolved and stir into the mousse.

When the mousse is on the point of setting, whisk the egg whites until stiff and whisk in the remaining sugar.

Fold the fromage frais into the mousse, then fold in the egg whites. Spoon the mousse into a serving bowl and refrigerate for 1–2 hours until set.

CRÈME CARAMEL

85 g/3 oz sugar
3 tablespoons water
4 eggs
550 ml/1 pint creamy milk
1 tablespoon sugar
½ teaspoon vanilla essence

I get the best results with crème caramel when I start with a cold oven, and allow everything to heat together.

Melt the 85 g/3 oz sugar in a heavy saucepan, stirring constantly until the caramel cooks to a mid brown. Remove from the heat and very carefully add the water. The caramel will bubble up. Stir well to allow all the caramel to dissolve, heating if necessary. Pour into a 1 litre/2 pint soufflé dish.

Beat the remaining ingredients together and strain over the caramel. Put the dish in 2.5 cm/1 inch cold water in a roasting pan. Put this in the oven, set it to 150°C/300°F/Gas 2 and cook for 75 minutes or until set.

Allow to cool, then invert into a deep serving dish.

PASSIONFRUIT SORBET
in ginger snap baskets

makes 10
115 g/4 oz sugar
220 ml/8 fl oz water
4 passionfruit
juice of 1 lemon

for the baskets
60 g/2 oz demerara sugar
60 g/2 oz golden syrup
60 g/2 oz butter
60 g/2 oz plain flour
1 teaspoon ground ginger
2 oranges, to shape the baskets

This dessert may be decorated with fresh fruit or flowers

First make the sorbet. In a medium saucepan dissolve the sugar in the water and bring to the boil. Cook for 4 minutes to make a syrup. Remove from the heat and allow to cool.

Cut the passionfruit in half and scrape the seeds into a sieve, pressing through as much juice as you can. Add the lemon juice and the syrup to the passionfruit juice and stir. Pour into a freezer container and freeze for 4–6 hours, stirring well with a fork every hour to break up the crystals.

For the ginger snap baskets, heat the oven to 160°C/325°F/Gas 3. Melt the sugar, syrup and butter in a saucepan and remove from the heat. Stir in the flour and ginger, mixing well. On a large greased baking sheet drop 2 dessertspoons of mixture well apart. Bake in the oven for 7–8 minutes, until golden brown.

Remove the tray from the oven and allow the ginger snaps to cool for a couple of minutes. Slip a palette knife under one biscuit and quickly and carefully lay it on top of an orange, moulding it slightly to fit. Flatten the bottom of the 'basket' by pressing on to a board and repeat with the other biscuit. You have sufficient mixture to make 10 baskets.

As soon as the baskets are cool, and while the next batch is cooking, remove them carefully from the oranges. Turn right side up and store in an airtight tin for up to 3 days.

15 minutes before serving, move the sorbet into the fridge to allow it to soften slightly. Place a basket on each plate and spoon in the sorbet. Decorate, if liked, with fresh fruit or flowers and serve.

MERINGUES

One of the paradoxes of life is that people who make mayonnaise tend not to make meringues, and vice versa. As there is not yet, to my knowledge, a support service dedicated to uniting all these separated whites and yolks, I suggest making this foolproof recipe for meringues, and the yolk-rich cake on page 26.

Note that homemade meringues are softer in texture and colour than the manufactured variety.

For each egg white you will need 60 g/2 oz caster sugar. I use an electric beater to whisk the mixture: the volume is slightly less, but the meringue is stiff and glossy.

Whisk the whites until stiff, then whisk in one third of the sugar. Beat at full speed for 1 minute, then add the next third. Beat for a further minute, then add the remaining sugar and continue to beat for 4–5 minutes, until the mixture is very stiff.

Spoon or pipe meringues about 5 cm/2 inches in diameter on to nonstick baking sheets and cook in a preheated oven at 150°C/300°F/Gas 2 for 1 hour. Larger meringues will take longer, small meringue kisses only about 45 minutes.

When the meringue is ready it should lift easily from the tray. Allow to cool on a rack, then store in an airtight tin.

PAVLOVA

3 large egg whites
170 g/6 oz caster sugar
1 teaspoon cornflour
1 teaspoon wine vinegar
275 ml/½ pint whipping cream
fresh fruit: banana, orange, mango etc.
2 passionfruit

Fresh fruit is the usual topping for Pavlova, with wonderfully flavoured passionfruit seeds spooned over.

Using an electric beater, beat the whites until stiff. Add the sugar one third at a time, continuing to beat until the mixture is stiff and glossy. Sift the cornflour over the surface of the meringue and sprinkle over the vinegar. With a metal spoon, carefully fold these into the meringue.

When thoroughly combined, spoon the mixture on to a piece of greaseproof paper on a baking sheet. Shape the meringue into an 18 cm/7 inch circle and hollow the centre slightly. Bake in a preheated oven at 140°C/275°F/Gas 1 for 75 minutes.

Allow to cool, carefully remove the greaseproof and serve topped with whipped cream and fruit. Spoon the passionfruit seeds over the top.

ALMOND AND CHERRY MERINGUE

5 egg whites
115 g/4 oz icing sugar
140 g/5 oz ground almonds
275 ml/½ pint double cream
140 ml/¼ pint thick yogurt or
**   soured cream**
1 tin cherry pie filling or
**   400 g/14 oz fresh berries**

Not quite as sweet as a classic meringue, this pudding transforms a standby tin of pie filling. Do use fresh berries if they are available, but remember that they may need extra sugar.

Whisk the egg whites until stiff and fold in the icing sugar and almonds. Have 3 well oiled baking sheets ready, divide the meringue between them, and spread into three 20 cm/8 inch circles. Bake in a preheated oven at 130°C/250°F/Gas ½ for 60 minutes or until crisp.

Carefully remove the meringues from the trays and allow to cool on wire racks. When the meringue is cold, whip the cream until quite stiff and fold in the yogurt or soured cream.

Place one circle of meringue on a serving dish and spread over the cream mixture. Place a second meringue on top. Cover this with the cherry pie filling or fresh berries and top with the final meringue. Dust the top with a little extra sugar and allow to sit for about 1 hour before serving.

BROWN SUGAR HAZELNUT MERINGUES

3 large egg whites
85 g/3 oz caster sugar
85 g/3 oz light muscovado sugar
60 g/2 oz ground hazelnuts

Hazelnuts and brown sugar make these chewy meringues a perfect way to use up leftover egg whites. Make small meringues to serve with coffee after dinner or larger ones to eat with fruit and cream.

Whip the egg whites with an electric beater until stiff but not dry. Add the caster sugar and continue to beat until the mixture is thick and glossy. Then add the brown sugar and beat for a further 2 minutes. Fold in the hazelnuts and spoon on to a well oiled baking sheet.

Bake in a cool oven at 130°C/250°F/Gas ½ for 1 hour or until crisp. Remove from the tray while still warm and allow to cool on a rack. Store in an airtight tin.

FRUIT PIZZA

225 g/8 oz plain flour
¼ teaspoon salt
½ teaspoon baking powder
60 g/2 oz butter
60 g/2 oz caster sugar
1 size 2 egg, beaten
½ teaspoon vanilla essence

for the topping
225 g/8 oz cream cheese
60 g/2 oz icing sugar
¼ teaspoon vanilla essence
900 g/2 lb mixed fruit:
  strawberries, raspberries,
  blueberries, sliced nectarines etc.

Really a fruit tart, this 'pizza' has a biscuit dough base and can be topped with any summer fruit available. If liked, it can be glazed with redcurrant jelly melted with a little water.

Sift together the flour, salt and baking powder. Cream the butter with the sugar, beat in the egg and vanilla and then mix in the flour. You should have a stiff dough. Chill for 30 minutes.

Roll out on a floured board to give a circle of dough about 20 cm/8 inches in diameter. Neaten the edges. Place on a baking sheet and cook in a preheated oven at 190°C/375°F/ Gas 5 for about 20 minutes, until lightly browned. Allow to cool.

Beat the cream cheese with the icing sugar and vanilla and spread over the cold base. Arrange the prepared fruit in circles until the whole is covered.

STRAWBERRY CHEESECAKE

200 g/7 oz ginger biscuits, crushed
60 g/2 oz butter, melted
340 g/12 oz cottage cheese
340 g/12 oz natural yogurt
85 g/3 oz caster sugar
¼ teaspoon almond essence
1 sachet gelatine
225 g/8 oz strawberries
2–3 tablespoons strawberry jam

This very light cheesecake doesn't contain raw eggs. As the cake is sliced the strawberries are discovered buried in the cream.

To make the base, mix the crushed biscuits with the butter and press into a loose bottomed 18 cm/ 7 inch cake tin. Put in the fridge until needed.

In a blender or food processor mix the cheese, yogurt, sugar and almond essence until smooth.

Sprinkle the gelatine over 3 tablespoons water and when swollen, heat gently to dissolve. Add this to the cheese and process to mix well. When the mixture thickens and begins to set, remove the prepared tin from the fridge and arrange the strawberries on the base. Carefully pour over the cheese mixture, pressing down any berries that float up to the surface.

Chill for 3–4 hours until firmly set. Just before serving, dip briefly into hot water and remove from the tin. Place the cheesecake on a serving dish and spread the jam over the top.

BLUEBERRY CHEESECAKE

225 g/8 oz plain chocolate digestive
  biscuits
85 g/3 oz butter, melted
1 tablespoon caster sugar
3 medium eggs
85 g/3 oz caster sugar
190 g/7 oz cream cheese
140 ml/¼ pint soured cream
1 tablespoon plain flour
grated rind and juice of ½ lemon

to finish
400 g/14 oz tin blueberries or other
  red fruit
2 teaspoons arrowroot

If you haven't a tin of blueberries to hand use cherries, raspberries or, of course, fresh fruit.

Crumble the biscuits, mix with the butter and the first quantity of sugar. Line the base of a 20 cm/ 8 inch springform tin with the mixture. Refrigerate for 1 hour.

Beat together the eggs, remaining sugar, cream cheese, cream, flour, lemon rind and juice. Beat until smooth, then pour on to the biscuit base. Bake the cheese-cake in a preheated oven at 190°C/ 375°F/Gas 5 for 30 minutes, or until the top is set. Allow to cool, then run a knife round the edge and remove from the tin.

Meanwhile, heat the blueberries in their juice to boiling point. Slake the arrowroot with water and stir into the hot fruit. Stirring gently, allow the mixture to boil for 30 seconds to thicken, then remove from the heat and allow to cool. Spoon on to the cheesecake.

LEMON AND ALMOND CHEESECAKE

225 g/8 oz shortcrust pastry
140 g/5 oz butter
170 g/6 oz curd cheese
140 g/5 oz caster sugar
140 g/5 oz ground almonds
45 g/1½ oz plain flour
grated rind and juice of 1 lemon
5 eggs, beaten
110 g/4 oz currants

This baked cheesecake manages to be wonderfully dense in texture without being too cloying.

Line a 20 cm/8 inch flan tin with the pastry. Preheat the oven to 220°C/425°F/Gas 7 with a metal baking tray on the middle shelf.

Beat the butter and cheese together until smooth, then beat in the sugar, almonds, flour, lemon rind and juice. Add the beaten egg a little at a time and mix in well. (This can be done in a food processor.) Stir in the currants and pour the mixture into the pastry case.

Bake in the oven on the preheated tray for 30 minutes, then turn the heat down to 190°C/375°F/Gas 5. Continue to cook for a further 15–25 minutes, until the cheesecake is a light golden brown and the pastry cooked.

Allow to cool on a rack, then remove from the tin.

If the currants sink to the bottom don't worry, the cheesecake will still be delicious.

CITRUS FRUIT
with Greek yogurt and honey

serves 4
1–2 large navel oranges
1 large pink fleshed grapefruit
30 g/1 oz slivered almonds
30 g/1 oz chopped hazelnuts
225 g/8 oz Greek yogurt
Greek flower honey (clear)

With a very sharp knife cut the rind and pith from the oranges and the grapefruit. Carefully cut the segments from the central membrane and arrange them on four plates. In a dry pan toast the nuts until they are a light golden brown. Divide the yogurt between the plates and sprinkle with the toasted nuts. Drizzle a little honey over each dish and hand more honey separately.

SAFFRON SCENTED YOGURT
with pink grapefruit

1 pinch saffron stems
2 tablespoons warm milk
sugar to taste
600 ml/1 pint thick creamy yogurt
3–4 Indian River grapefruit

Pink fleshed Indian River grapefruit are much sweeter than the yellow fleshed ones.

Place the saffron in a long handled kitchen spoon and toast over a medium flame until it just begins to change colour. Crush to a powder and stir into the warm milk, mixing until well dissolved. Stir this milk and sugar to taste into the yogurt.

Using a sharp knife, cut all the peel and pith from the grapefruit. Cut the individual segments from the fruit and arrange on a platter with the bowl of yogurt in the centre. Sprinkle with sugar if liked.

BAKED LEMON PUDDING

115 g/4 oz butter
grated rind and juice of 2 lemons
170 g/6 oz caster sugar
4 eggs, separated
415 ml/¾ pint milk
2 tablespoons plain flour

This deliciously light lemon pudding separates into two layers as it cooks.

I use a food processor for the first stage. Cream the butter, lemon rind and sugar until you have a light mixture. Add the yolks, lemon juice, flour and milk and process or beat well.

Beat the egg whites to a stiff glossy foam, then fold in the lemon mixture. Pour into a greased ovenproof serving dish and bake in a roasting tin with 2.5 cm/1 inch hot water for 60–65 minutes. The top will be mid brown and may crack slightly.

STEAMED GINGER, LEMON AND SYRUP PUDDING

115 g/4 oz caster sugar
115 g/4 oz butter
2 size 3 eggs, beaten
115 g/4 oz self-raising flour
1 teaspoon ground ginger
grated rind and juice of ½ lemon
2 tablespoons syrup

A good old-fashioned steamed sponge pudding is just the thing for a cold autumn day.

Cream the sugar and butter until light, then beat in the egg, a little at a time. Fold in the flour, ginger and lemon rind.

Put the syrup and lemon juice into a 900 ml/1½ pint pudding basin and spoon the sponge mixture on top. Cover the basin tightly with foil or greaseproof and steam the pudding in a saucepan one third full of simmering water for 1½ hours.

Serve with soured cream or Greek yogurt.

LEMON, LEXIA RAISIN AND RUM PUDDING

60 g/2 oz raisins (lexia if possible)
2 tablespoons rum
115 g/4 oz soft butter
115 g/4 oz caster sugar
2 size 2 eggs
140 g/5 oz selfraising flour
grated rind of 1 scrubbed lemon

Soak the raisins in the rum for as long as possible, overnight is best. Make a sponge by creaming the butter with the sugar and adding the egg a little at a time. Fold in the flour, lemon zest, raisins and rum.

Spoon the mixture into a greased 900 ml/1½ pint pudding basin and cover the top with greaseproof paper, folding a pleat in the centre. Cover the paper with foil. Tie down with string and put the pudding in a deep pan one third full of boiling water. It is best to stand the basin on a trivet in the saucepan to stop the pudding scorching. Cover the pan and simmer the sponge for about 1½ hours.

Serve with cream.

LEMON MERINGUE RICE PUDDING

butter for the dish
550 ml/1 pint creamy milk
45 g/1½ oz pudding rice
30 g/1 oz caster sugar
2–3 large pieces lemon rind
2 eggs, separated
3 tablespoons lemon curd
85 g/3 oz caster sugar

Grease a shallow ovenproof dish and pour in the milk, rice, the first quantity of sugar and the lemon rind. Place in a preheated oven at 160°C/325°F/Gas 3 and bake, stirring occasionally, for about 1 hour, until the rice is tender. Remove from the oven and stir in the egg yolks one at a time, mixing well. The rice will thicken slightly. Allow to cool.

When the rice is cold, carefully spread the lemon curd over the top. Beat the egg whites until stiff, then beat in the remaining sugar. Spread the meringue over the pudding and bake in a preheated oven at 160°C/325°F/Gas 3 for 20–30 minutes, until the meringue is well risen and golden brown.

Serve warm.

SPOTTED DICK
with hot spiced cream

115 g/4 oz suet
115 g/4 oz self-raising flour
60 g/2 oz ground almonds
60 g/2 oz stale cake or white
  breadcrumbs
85 g/3 oz raisins, preferably
  muscatel
3 tablespoons soft brown sugar
1 egg, beaten
a squeeze of lemon juice
about 150 ml/¼ pint milk to mix

for the spiced cream
270 ml/½ pint double cream
2 teaspoons ground ginger
2 teaspoons powdered cinnamon
2 tablespoons soft brown sugar

Combine all the ingredients for the pudding in a bowl, mixing to a firm but moist consistency. Put the mixture into a greased 1 litre/ 2 pint pudding basin, cover with 2 rounds of greaseproof paper and then with either foil or a pudding cloth. Secure with string.

Steam the pudding for 2 hours in a saucepan half filled with hot water. Make sure the water is kept at a simmer and don't let the saucepan boil dry. Turn out carefully on to a dish.

To make the spiced cream, put all the ingredients in a nonstick saucepan and bring to the boil. Simmer, stirring constantly for 2–3 minutes. The cream will thicken slightly.

Serve the hot pudding with the hot cream.

SPICED RICE PUDDING

85 g/3 oz pudding rice
1 litre/2 pints creamy milk
85 g/3 oz sugar
seeds from 3 cardamom pods,
  crushed
1 blade mace
5 cm/2 inches cinnamon stick
a knob of butter

This rice pudding is spiced with cardamom and mace, giving it a wonderful Eastern flavour.

Grease a deep baking dish. Pour in all the ingredients and stir. Dot with butter and bake in a pre-heated oven at 150°C/300°F/ Gas 2 for 1½–2 hours, stirring occasionally.

Don't stir for the last 30 minutes to allow a skin to form. Be careful not to eat the whole spices!

FRUIT BREAD AND BUTTER PUDDING

170 g/6 oz two-day-old fruit loaf
butter
3 eggs, beaten
550 ml/1 pint creamy milk
3 tablespoons caster sugar
grated nutmeg

Slice the loaf fairly thinly and butter lightly. Cut each slice into 4 triangles and arrange them overlapping in a greased ovenproof dish, points uppermost. Beat the eggs with the milk and strain the mixture over the bread. The tips of the bread triangles should stick up out of the custard. Leave in a cool place for 1 hour.

Preheat the oven to 160°C/325°F/Gas 3. Just before cooking, sprinkle the sugar and nutmeg over the surface of the pudding. Place the pudding dish inside a roasting tin with 2.5 cm/1 inch water and bake the pudding for 50 minutes. The top should be golden brown and the points of bread crisp. Serve warm.

CHOCOLATE BREAD PUDDING

4 tablespoons cocoa powder
4 tablespoons boiling water
340 g/12 oz breadcrumbs (mixed
  brown and white)
2 size 2 eggs, beaten
300 ml/½ pint milk
60 g/2 oz butter, melted
170 g/6 oz soft brown sugar
115 g/4 oz chopped walnuts
1 teaspoon cinnamon
grated rind of 1 well scrubbed
  orange
demerara sugar for sprinkling

Mix the cocoa with the boiling water until you have a smooth paste. Combine all the ingredients, stirring well. Allow to sit for 1 hour.

Pour into a well greased shallow ovenproof dish and level the top. Sprinkle with demerara sugar and bake in a preheated oven at 180°C/360°F/Gas 4 for 45 minutes, or until the top is crisp.

Serve with cream.

FRESH PEACH AND CINNAMON SPONGE PUDDING

4 medium peaches
115 g/4 oz soft margarine
115 g/4 oz light muscovado sugar
2 medium eggs
115 g/4 oz wholemeal flour
1½ teaspoons baking powder
1½ teaspoons ground cinnamon

for the topping
1 tablespoon light muscovado
  sugar
1 teaspoon ground cinnamon

Fresh peaches make this wholemeal sponge moist and delicious.

Skin the peaches by covering with boiling water for 60 seconds, remove the stones, then chop into 1 cm/½ inch cubes. Put all the remaining ingredients except the topping into a bowl and beat well. Stir in the peach cubes and pour the batter into a greased 900 ml/ 1½ pint ovenproof dish.

Mix the sugar and cinnamon for the topping and sprinkle over the pudding. Bake in a preheated oven at 200°C/400°F/Gas 6 for 25–30 minutes, or until well risen and golden brown.

Serve warm with cream.

QUEEN OF PUDDINGS

30 g/1 oz butter
415 ml/¾ pint milk
grated rind of 1 lemon
115 g/4 oz crustless white bread,
  broken into 2.5 cm/1 inch pieces
1½ tablespoons caster sugar
3 egg yolks, beaten
2 tablespoons raspberry jam

for the topping
3 egg whites
85 g/3 oz caster sugar

This traditional favourite is made from ingredients readily found in the kitchen.

Melt the butter in the milk in a saucepan. Remove from the heat and stir in the lemon rind, bread and sugar. Mix to soften the bread and when smooth, stir in the egg yolks.

Pour into a buttered 1 litre/ 2 pint pie dish and bake in a preheated oven at 180°C/360°F/ Gas 4 for about 30 minutes. When the mixture is set, remove from the oven and spread over the jam.

For the topping, beat the egg whites with the sugar until thick and glossy, then either pipe or spread the meringue over the jam layer. Return to the oven and cook for about 15 minutes, until the mixture is browned. Serve warm.

AUTUMN FRUIT COBBLER

**900 g/2 lb prepared weight mixed
  fruit (apples, pears, plums etc.)**
4 tablespoons orange juice
sugar to taste

for the topping
170 g/6 oz plain flour
1 teaspoon baking powder
60 g/2 oz butter
60 g/2 oz sugar
1 teaspoon ground cinnamon
milk to mix

to finish
milk
demerara sugar

Cut the prepared fruit into pieces
of roughly even size and place in a
greased ovenproof dish. If you are
using rather hard pears, poach
them in the orange juice for 5–10
minutes before adding to the rest.
Add the juice and sugar to taste.

To make the cobbler topping,
sift the flour with the baking
powder and rub in the butter. Mix
in the sugar and cinnamon and
enough milk to give a soft but
manageable dough. Turn this out
on to a floured board and knead
lightly into a ball. Pat or roll out to
2 cm/¾ inch thick and cut into
5 cm/2 inch circles. Arrange these
on the fruit, brush with milk and
sprinkle with a little demerara
sugar.

Bake in a preheated oven at
180°C/360°F/Gas 4 for 30–40
minutes. Serve hot with ice cream.

OAT AND SESAME PLUM CRUMBLE

675 g/1½ lb ripe plums
60 g/2 oz medium oats
170 g/6 oz plain flour
85 g/3 oz soft butter
115 g/4 oz caster sugar
1 tablespoon sesame seeds

Cut the washed plums into
quarters and arrange them in a
shallow ovenproof dish, then pour
over 3 tablespoons water. Mix the
oats and flour together and rub in
the butter until you have a rough
crumble. Toss in the sugar and
sesame seeds and carefully sprinkle
the mixture over the plums.

Bake the crumble in a preheated
oven at 180°C/360°F/Gas 4 for
40–50 minutes, or until the top is
light brown. Serve warm with
single cream.

BAKED APPLES
with cranberries

**3 medium eating apples, cored and
diced
1 box fresh cranberries
85 g/3 oz caster sugar**

for the topping
**115 g/4 oz oatmeal
60 g/2 oz plain flour
60 g/2 oz brown sugar
60 g/2 oz butter**

Place the apples, cranberries and
sugar in a well greased ovenproof dish to a depth of about
8 cm/3 inches. Mix together the
topping ingredients and sprinkle
over the fruit. Dot with butter and
bake in a preheated oven at
180°C/360°F/Gas 4 for 35–40
minutes.

BAKED MUESLI-STUFFED APPLES
with honey and soured cream

**4 medium cooking apples
1–2 tablespoons light muscovado
sugar
1 teacup muesli
3 tablespoons clear honey
1 tablespoon butter
275 ml/½ pint water
140 ml/¼ pint soured cream**

Core the washed apples and score
a line around the centre of each
one. Mix the sugar with the cereal
and stuff the apples, arranging
them in an ovenproof dish. Spoon
over the honey and top each apple
with a knob of butter. Pour in the
water.

Bake the apples in a preheated
oven at 190°C/375°F/Gas 5 for
50–60 minutes, basting from time
to time with the collected juice.
Serve the apples hot topped with a
spoonful of soured cream.

Marmalade apple charlotte

115 g/4 oz butter
115 g/4 oz soft brown sugar
**225 g/8 oz stale breadcrumbs
(preferably granary)**
**900 g/2 lb cooking apples, peeled,
cored and sliced**
**2 tablespoons marmalade, or juice
and grated rind of 1 orange**

*When last year's cooking apples
start to lose their bite I like to use
a little marmalade or orange juice
to add zest.*

Melt the butter in a saucepan, then
stir in the sugar and breadcrumbs.
Grease an ovenproof dish and put
in the apple slices, dot them with
the marmalade and top with the
buttery crumbs. Bake in a preheated oven at 180°C/360°F/Gas 4
for 1 hour.
Serve warm with cream.

Baked Alaska

serves 8
**1 18 cm/7 inch diameter sponge
cake**
2 tablespoons orange liqueur
3 egg whites
170 g/6 oz caster sugar
**fruit of choice e.g. apricots in
brandy, strawberries, peach
slices**
825 ml/1½ pints vanilla ice cream

Put a metal plate large enough to
take the sponge in the freezer.
Sprinkle the sponge with the
liqueur.
Heat the oven to 200°C/400°F/
Gas 6.
Just before serving whisk the egg
whites until stiff, then beat in the
sugar, whisking until you have a
firm mousse.
Place the sponge on the cold
plate and spoon the chosen fruit
on top. Pile the ice cream over the
fruit in an even layer. Now cover
the whole thing, cake and all, with
the meringue, making sure there
are no gaps. For special occasions
pipe on the meringue.
Place the Alaska in the oven and
cook for 4–5 minutes until the
meringue is lightly browned. Serve
at once.

TOSCA APPLES

4 tart apples, peeled, cored and halved
85 g/3 oz caster sugar
1 tablespoon plain flour
60 g/2 oz butter
1 tablespoon milk
45 g/1½ oz flaked almonds

This Swedish pudding is deliciously different and simple to make.

Place the apples, cut side down, in a baking dish.

Mix the sugar, flour, butter and milk in a saucepan and simmer over a low heat until the sauce is smooth, stirring constantly. Mix in the almonds and pour this sauce over the fruit.

Bake in a preheated oven at 180°C/360°F/Gas 4 for 20–25 minutes, until the apples are tender and the sauce lightly browned.

SCANDINAVIAN APPLE PUDDING

140 g/5 oz brown breadcrumbs
2 very large cooking apples
140 g/5 oz soft brown sugar
45 g/1½ oz butter

This apple pudding is somewhat lighter than most as it contains very little butter.

Grease a 20 cm/8 inch cake tin and line with a circle of greaseproof paper. Sprinkle one third of the crumbs over the base of the tin. Peel and core one apple, then finely slice it over the crumbs. Sprinkle on one third of the sugar.

Now layer on more crumbs, apple and sugar, finishing with a layer of sugar-sprinkled crumbs. Dot the top with the butter and bake in a preheated oven at 180°C/360°F/Gas 4 for 45 minutes, or until the top is a rich golden brown.

Serve hot with cream or allow to cool, then remove carefully from the tin.

DATE AND NUT UPSIDE-DOWN PUDDING

grated rind and juice of 1 scrubbed
   orange
30 g/1 oz butter
30 g/1 oz light muscovado sugar
60 g/2 oz chopped nuts
60 g/2 oz chopped, stoned dates
115 g/4 oz butter
115 g/4 oz light muscovado sugar
2 size 2 eggs, beaten
115 g/4 oz self-raising flour

I always seem to have an odd assortment of nuts and a few dates left over after Christmas. This upside-down pudding uses them up under a chewy toffee topping.

Mix together the orange juice and the first quantities of butter and sugar, and spread in the base of a deep 20 cm/8 inch cake tin. Sprinkle over the nuts and dates.

Cream the second quantities of butter and sugar with the orange zest, and beat until light and fluffy. Add the egg a little at a time, then fold in the flour.

Spoon this mixture carefully over the nuts and bake in a preheated oven at 180°C/360°F/Gas 4 for 30–35 minutes, until risen and golden brown. The pudding is done when it starts to pull slightly from the sides of the tin. Invert the tin on to a serving plate and allow to sit for 2–3 minutes. Remove the tin and serve the pudding hot with soured cream.

NECTARINE AND BLUEBERRY BAKE

5–6 large nectarines
170 g/6 oz blueberries
85 g/3 oz plain flour
115 g/4 oz soft brown sugar
60 g/2 oz porridge oats
½ teaspoon salt
1 teaspoon cinnamon
85 g/3 oz butter

I like to bake nectarines and peaches in pies and crumbles, or under this crisp topping of brown sugar, spices and oats.

Slice the nectarines into an ovenproof dish, discarding the stones. Toss in the blueberries.

Mix together the remaining ingredients, rubbing in the butter until the mixture looks like breadcrumbs. (This can be done in a food processor.) Sprinkle the topping evenly over the fruit and bake in a preheated oven at 190°C/375°F/Gas 5 for 40–50 minutes or until the top is golden brown and crisp.

Serve warm with cream.

APRICOT AND ALMOND SOUFFLÉ PANCAKES

makes 8–10
150 g/5½ oz plain flour
60 g/2 oz soft butter
60 g/2 oz caster sugar
3 size 2 eggs, separated
1 teaspoon vanilla essence
440 ml/16 fl oz milk

to finish
30 g/1 oz ground almonds
30 g/1 oz icing sugar
about 85 g/3 oz butter for cooking
apricot jam

Mix the ground almonds with the icing sugar for the topping and reserve.

Beat together the flour, butter, sugar, egg yolks, vanilla and milk until smooth. Whisk the egg whites to a firm but not dry snow and fold in to the batter.

Heat an 18 cm/7 inch frying pan and when hot put in 1 teaspoon butter. As soon as the butter has melted, pour in sufficient batter to give a pancake about 5 mm/¼ inch deep. Cook the pancake over a moderate heat until bubbles rise to the surface and begin to burst.

Turn the pancake and cook for a few seconds to set the other side. Turn the cooked pancake on to a board and spread with apricot jam. Fold in half and place in an ovenproof dish, then sprinkle with a little of the almond mixture.

Continue to cook and fill the pancake until all the butter is used. You should have 8–10 pancakes. Sprinkle any remaining sugar and almond mixture over the dish and reheat for 15–20 minutes in a preheated oven at 150°C/300°F/ Gas 2.

Serve with fresh or soured cream.

Hot chocolate soufflé

115 g/4 oz plain chocolate
4 tablespoons double cream
4 large eggs, separated
2 tablespoons brandy
2 or 3 Amoretti biscuits, optional
caster sugar and butter for the dish

Sweet soufflés are ambrosial. They can be served at a dinner party, but I prefer to keep them to spoil my family or a very few close friends, as they do need a little preparation just before cooking and the timing can be tricky to fit into a formal meal. Chocolate has sufficient body not to need a sauce base, and you can bury a few liqueur-soaked Amoretti biscuits under the mixture for extra dash.

Melt the chocolate with the cream over a pan of hot water or in a microwave, then beat in the yolks one at a time. Add the brandy and crumbled Amoretti biscuits if used.

Butter a straight sided dish about 18 cm/7 inches across, and sprinkle the inside with caster sugar. Heat the oven to 200°C/400°F/Gas 6.

Beat the egg whites until stiff and glossy, then fold them quickly and lightly into the chocolate mixture. Pour the mixture into the prepared dish and bake for 25–30 minutes. The soufflé will be soft in the middle.

Orange liqueur soufflé

butter and sugar for the dish
1 medium orange
2–3 tablespoons orange brandy
45 g/1½ oz butter
45 g/1½ oz plain flour
275 ml/½ pint milk
85 g/3 oz caster sugar
4 size 2 eggs, separated

Butter an 18 cm/7 inch soufflé dish and sprinkle with sugar.

Grate the zest from the well washed orange, remove the remaining peel and chop the flesh into 1 cm/½ inch cubes. Put the orange chunks into the prepared dish and pour over 1 tablespoon brandy.

Make a thick white sauce with the butter, flour and milk, and simmer for 2–3 minutes, then stir in the caster sugar. Remove from the heat, and add the egg yolks one at a time, beating well between each addition. The mixture will thicken slightly. Add the remaining orange brandy and the orange zest.

Allow to cool for a few minutes. (You can prepare up to this point 2–3 hours ahead, provided you cover the surface of the sauce with cling film to prevent a skin forming. Re-heat gently before continuing.)

Beat the whites until stiff and fold into the orange mixture. Pour into the prepared dish and bake for 25–30 minutes. The soufflé will be well risen, golden brown and soft in the middle.

SOUFFLÉ AUX NOIX

makes 4 small or 1 large soufflé
butter and sugar for the dishes
4 sponge finger biscuits
1–2 tablespoons liqueur de noix or
 brandy
4 size 2 eggs, separated
4 tablespoons caster sugar
60 g/2 oz walnut kernels, finely
 ground

A napkin may be wrapped round each dish just before serving to make handling easier.

Butter 4 individual soufflé dishes 10 cm/4 inches in diameter or one 18 cm/7 inch dish, and sprinkle the sides and base with caster sugar. In a separate bowl break the biscuits into pieces and pour on the liqueur.

Beat the yolks with the caster sugar until pale. Whip the whites until stiff but not dry. Fold the ground walnuts into the yolks, then fold this into the stiff egg whites.

Divide half the mixture between the dishes, add the soaked biscuits and top with the remaining mixture. Bake in a preheated oven at 200°C/400°F/Gas 6 for 15 minutes, and serve at once with a little single cream.

CHOCOLATE AND ALMOND SOUFFLÉ

serves 2
2 large eggs, separated
1½ tablespoons caster sugar
60 g/2 oz plain chocolate
30 g/1 oz ground almonds
1 tablespoon brandy
butter and sugar for the dishes
150 ml/¼ pint single cream

Beat the yolks with the sugar until you have a pale light mass. Melt the chocolate over a bowl of hot water and reserve. Whisk the whites until stiff but not dry.

Fold the almonds, brandy and chocolate into the mousse carefully and thoroughly.

Divide the mixture between two buttered sugared 10 cm/4 inch soufflé dishes, and bake in a preheated oven at 200°C/400°F/Gas 6 for 15–20 minutes, until well risen.

Remove from the oven and allow to cool. Run a knife around the soufflés and turn on to an ovenproof serving dish. Cover with cling film and refrigerate until needed.

When ready to serve, pour the cream over the soufflés and reheat for 10–15 minutes in a preheated oven at 160°C/325°F/Gas 3.

INDEX

Index